Memories of Westgate

by
MARGARET JACKSON

A WESTGATE FAMILY CIRCA 1930

Memory is the Treasury of all things

With grateful thanks to:
Janet & Ron Bye for their unfailing encouragement of this project
and John Jackson for his help through the 'computer maze'.

CONTENTS

Published by youbooks.co.uk
11 Riverside Park, Sheaf Gardens, Sheffield S2 4BB
Telephone 0114 275 7222
www.youbooks.co.uk

Printed by
Pickards.org.uk

Introduction

Westgate, until the 1950's, was a busy thriving area. In the nineteenth century it was a main transportation route and nearby industry was well served by the adjacent River Don.

There was a mix of houses, courts and slums, trades, professions and shops. Westgate had chapels and schools and was well known for its public houses.

Westgate was a community.

Reproduced by kind permission of Rotherham Family History Society

This view is looking up Westgate towards The Co-op on the left with the Imperial Buildings top centre and the spire of All Saints in the distance. The buildings on the right with the attics are still visible today.

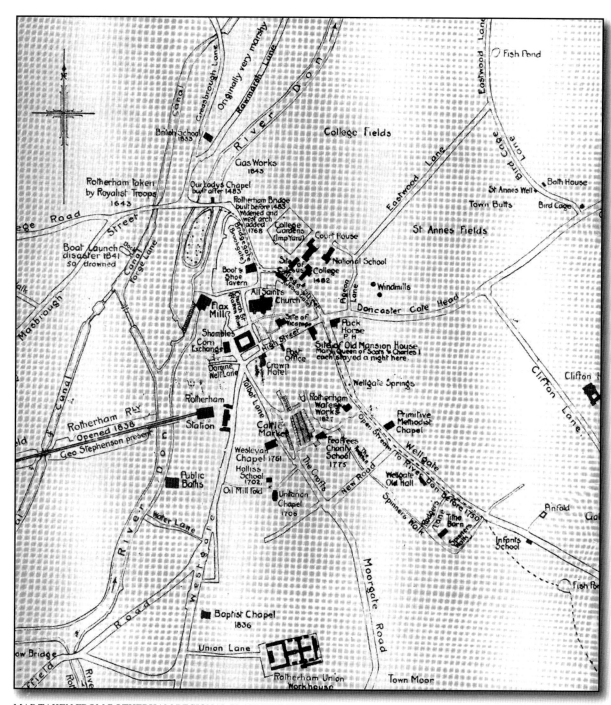

MAP TAKEN FROM ROTHERHAM REGIONAL PLANNING SCHEME 1925

One

Occupants of Westgate
Their Trades & Professions
1862

Emily Edwards [nee Needham] Born 1858

OCCUPANTS OF WESTGATE 1862

George Barnby	Tailor & Draper	16 & 88 Westgate
Martha Barton	Day School	81 Westgate
James Bennett	Plumber, Glazier Gasfitter	14 Westgate
Robert John Bentley	Ale & Porter Brewer & Maltster	Rotherham Old Brewery Westgate [Home- West End & Finningley Park]
Mrs Ann Booth	-	Westgate Green
Michael Bradshaw	Poulterer	75 Westgate
George Bridge	Stove Grate Manufacturer	Baptist Chapel Lane Westgate [Home] Clifton Terrace
Elizabeth Brooke	Greengrocer	4 Westgate
William Brookes	Engineer	2 Prospect Place Westgate
Geo Burrell & Sons	Boot & Shoemaker	Westgate & Change Alley Sheffield
John Chislett	Bookkeeper	98 Westgate
John Clapson	Shopkeeper & Veterinary Surgeon	39 Westgate
John Clarke	Land Agent & Agent to West Riding Trade Protection Society	21 Westgate
William Clarke	MD & Surgeon	9 Westgate
Joseph Richardson Clayton	Ironmonger	13 Westgate
William Clifford	Brewers Manager	Westgate
Francis Colley	Victualler Station Inn	18 Westgate
Thomas Cooper	Joiner	Near Dusty Miller, Westgate
Charles Copley	Shopkeeper	57 Westgate
Charles Leach Coward	Solicitor	6 Westgate [work] [Home] South Grove
Joseph Crossby	Corn & Flour Dealer	50 Westgate
John Dawson	Drapers Assistant	79 Westgate
John Dickinson	Shopkeeper	69 Westgate
John Dickinson	Nail Manufacturer	Westgate
James Dobb	Victualler Dusty Miller	Westgate
Michael Dunn	Shoemaker	47 Westgate
Joseph Easton	Plumber, Glazier Gasfitter	23 Westgate
John Evans	Hairdresser + Hatter	10 Westgate
Miss Elizabeth Favell	-	4 Prospect Place, Westgate
Thomas Vickers Favell	Solicitor	39 Westgate [Home] Wheathill House
William Favell	Nail Manufacturer	51 Westgate
Martha Gillatt	Hatter	3 Westgate
Henry Goodinson	Brassfounder	Baptist Chapel Lane Westgate

Joseph Green	Grocer	53 Westgate
Thomas Gregory	Cabinet Makers	41 Westgate
Mr Edward Griffiths		Water Lane, Westgate
George Hague	Grocer & Flour Dealer	7 Westgate
Richard Hague	General Dealer	73 Westgate
William Hallam	Shopkeeper	72 Westgate
William Hanby	Grocer	70 Westgate
William Hanby	Beerhouse	49 Westgate
James Hattersley	Rope & Net Manufacturer	140 Westgate
James Hattersley Jnr	Joiner & Builder	Water Lane [Home]-140 Westgate
Arthur Hirst	Manager for Robert John Bentley Esq	The Mount Westgate
William Hirst	Solicitor	25 Westgate
James Hodgson	Corn Merchant & Miller	Rotherham Mills, Westgate [Home] West End, Westgate
Wiliam Fretwell Hoyle	Solicitor, Registrar of County Court, Agent to Atlas Fire & Life& Albert Fire Offices, Steward to the Manor, Clerk to Tinsley & Doncaster, Sheffield & Tinsley, Rotherham & Swinton, Rotherham Barnby Moor & Rotherham & Pleasley Turnpike Roads.	Westgate [Home] Ferham House
Joseph Hutton	Beerhouse	58 Westgate
Hannah Jackson	Victualler White Swann	71 Westgate
John Kerr	Linen & Wool Draper	1 Westgate [Home] Moorgate
Rupert Lomas	Hawker	66 Westgate
Matthew George Mallinson	Cab Owner & Victualler Ship Inn	2 Westgate
Marsh & Edwards	Solicitors, Agents to Yorkshire Fire & Life Office & to	8 Westgate
Robert Marsh Junior	Solicitor Marsh & Edwards & Perpetual Commissioner, Midland counties Hail & Storm Co & Solicitors to Rotherham Agricultural Association	[Home] The Ickles
John Martin	Greengrocer	102 Westgate
Richard Martin	Victualler True Briton	78 Westgate
Charles Morris	Mason + Builder & Grocer	Talbot Lane 17 Westgate
Hannah Morris	Straw Bonnet Maker	114 Westgate
William Myers	Tailor	1Prospect Place, Westgate
Mary Ann Nadin	Shopkeeper	61 Westgate

George Neatby	Iron & Brassfounder Railway Foundry	Westgate
George Neatby	Beerhouse Keeper	27 Westgate
Sarah Newton	Chemist &Druggist	11 Westgate
Edward Nightingale	Grocer & Tallow Chandler	9 Westgate
Thomas O' Brien	Beerhouse Keeper	22 Westgate
Ellen Outram	Cow Keeper	84 Westgate
Joseph Roger Owen	Postmaster	5 Westgate
Oxley Elizabeth	-	28 Westgate
Edward Pagden	Gentleman	42 Westgate
Francis Parker	Land Agent & Auditor of Accounts & Agent to Scottish Union Fire & Life Office	16 Westgate [Home]- Eastwood Villa
George Parkin	Carrier to Sheffield	Westgate
Thomas Parkin	Maltster	Westgate & Sheffield
Payne Brother	General Brassfounder & Manufacturers of all kinds of Plumbers Brass Works	86 Westgate
James Payne	Brassfounder & Co [Payne Bros]	[Home] - 86 Westgate
Robert Poulter	Victualler Wellington Inn	52 Westgate
Sarah Ramsbottom	Mistress Hollis Free School	Oil Mill Fold Westgate
William Raper	Cabinet Maker	92 Westgate
Mary Ann Reynolds	Shopkeeper	55 Westgate
William Henry Rising	Solicitor & Agent to Liverpool & London Fire & Life Office	12 Westgate [Home]- Crofts
Edward Robinson	Surgeon	West Ville, Westgate
Thomas Rodgers	Cooper & Greengrocer	56 Westgate
Dalby Scoons	Inland Revenue Officer & Corn Inspector	124 Westgate
Amelia Smith	Shopkeeper	35 Westgate
Henry Smith	Maltster, Brewer & Shopkeeper	43 Westgate
Henry T Smith	Smallware Dealer	45 Westgate
John Steane	Master of British School [Rawmarsh Road]	126 Westgate
John Steer	Beerhouse Keeper	80 Westgate
John Taylor	Miller	5 Prospect Place Westgate
Mrs Elizabeth Thompson	-	134 Westgate
George Thompson	Cow Keeper	85 Westgate
Joseph Thompson	Cow Keeper	83 Westgate
Henry Tomlinson	Ironfounder & Stove Grate Manufacturer Bath Foundry	Westgate [Home] Orchard House Victoria St Masbro'
Ann Turner	Shopkeeper	138 Westgate
Henry Turner	Station Master	19 Westgate

Daniel Charles Wheatley	Corn Merchant	Water Lane, Westgate
		[Home] Elmfield, Alma Road
Mrs Mary Wigfield		44 Westgate
William Wilkinson	Coach Builder-College Yard	
	Eating House	40 Westgate
William Wilkinson	Manager	130 Westgate
Benjamin Charles Williams	- Medical Botanist	37 Westgate
George Williams	Shoemaker	35 Westgate
George Williams	Shoemaker	38 Westgate
		[Home] - Wellgate
Samuel Wintle	Shopkeeper	76 Westgate
Ann & Elizabeth Wood	Dressmakers	34 Westgate
Henry Wood	Victualler Cutlers Arms	31 Westgate
George Woollen	Plumber, Glazier & Gasfitter Masbro' St	[Home] 46 Westgate
William Worth	Rope, Twine & Net Manufacturers & Dealer In Sacking, Cart Sheets & Covers	26 Westgate
John Wright	Blacksmith- Canal Wharf	[Home]- Westgate

Trades and Professions - Westgate 1862

ACADEMIES

Martha Barton   81 Westgate

ATTORNEYS

Charles Leach Coward   6 Westgate
Thomas Vickers Favell   30 Westgate
William Hirst   25 Westgate
William Fretwell Hoyle   20 Westgate
Marsh & Edwards   8 Westgate
William Henry Rising   12 Westgate

BOOT & SHOE MAKERS

G Burrell & Son   Westgate
Michael Dunn   47 Westgate
George Williams   38 Westgate

BRASS FOUNDERS

Henry Goodinson   Baptist Chapel Lane
                            Westgate
Payne Brothers   86 Westgate

BRAZIERS, TINNERS & IRONMONGERS

J.R. Clayton   13 Westgate

BREWERS, ALE & PORTER

Robert John Bentley   Rotherham Old
                            Brewery Westgate
Henry Smith   43 Westgate

CATTLE DEALERS

Robert Spendlove   48 Westgate

CHEMIST & DRUGGIST

Sarah Newton   11 Westgate

COAL DEALERS

Charlotte Steer   Yard
                            78 Westgate
Thomas Woodhouse [merchant]
                            Railway yard
                            Westgate

COOPERS

Thomas Rodgers   56 Westgate

CORN, SEED & TILLAGE MERCHANTS

Joseph Crossby   50 Westgate

EATING & COFFEE HOUSES
& IRONMONGERS

William Wilkinson   40 Westgate

FLOUR DEALER

J.J. Goodwin   Westgate
James Hodgson   Rotherham Mills Westgate

                            [home West End]

FIRE & LIFE OFFICERS

W F Hoyle   20 Westgate
Albert Life & Atlas
John Clarke   21 Westgate
British Mutual Life
TV Favell   30 Westgate
Rock Life
Marsh & Edwards   8 Westgate
Midland Counties Hail,
Storm & Yorkshire
Francis Parker   16 Westgate
Scottish Union

GREENGROCERS

Elizabeth Brook   4 Westgate
John Martin   102 Westgate
Thomas Rodgers   56 Westgate

GROCERS & TEA DEALERS

Joseph Green   53 Westgate
George Hague   7 Westgate
William Hanby   70 Westgate
Charles Morris   17 Westgate
Edward Nightingale   9 Westgate
[also Tallow Chandler]

HAIR DRESSERS

John Evans   10 Westgate

HATTERS

John Evans   10 Westgate

HERBALIST

Benjamin Charles
Williams   37 Westgate

HORSE & GIG LETTERS
+CAB PROPRIETORS

+Mathew Mallinson   2 Westgate

HOSIERS

A&M Green   45 Westgate
Henry Smith   Westgate

HOTELS, INNS & TAVERNS

Henry Wood	Cutlers Arms 31 Westgate
James Dobb	Dusty Miller Westgate
George Matthew Mallinson	Ship Hotel 2 Westgate
Francis Colley	Station Inn, 18 Westgate
Richard Martin	True Briton 78 Westgate
Robert Poulter	Wellington 50 Westgate
H Jackson	White Swan 71 Westgate

BEER HOUSES

William Hanby	49 Westgate
Joseph Hutton	58 Westgate
George Neatby	27 Westgate
John Steer	80 Westgate

IRON FOUNDERS, ENGINEERS MILLWRIGHTS +STOVE GRATE MANUFACTURERS

+George Bridge	Baptist Chapel Lane, Westgate
+George Neatby	Railway Foundry Westgate
+Henry Tomlinson	Bath Foundry

IRONMONGERS

Joseph Richardson Clayton	13 Westgate

JOINERS & BUILDERS

James Hattersley	Water Lane
Charles Morris	17 Westgate

LAND & ESTATE AGENTS

John Clarke	21 Westgate
Francis Parker [& Auditor of Accounts]	16 Westgate

LINEN & WOOLLEN DRAPERS

John Kerr	1 Westgate

MALTSTERS + BREWERS

+Robert John Bentley	Rotherham Old Brewery, Westgate
Thomas Parkin	Westgate
+Henry Smith	43 Westgate

MILLINERS & DRESSMAKERS+ STRAW BONNET MAKER

A&M Green	45 Westgate
Ann & Elizabeth Wood	34 Westgate
+Hannah Morris	114 Westgate

NAILMAKERS

John Dickinson	Westgate
William Favell	51 Westgate
George Woollen	Westgate & Masbro Street

PAINTERS

George Woollen	Westgate & Masbro Street

PHYSICIANS/+ SURGEONS

+William Clarke	9 Westgate
+Edward Robinson	Westgate

PLASTERERS CEMENT DEALERS

Moses Harris	53 Westgate

PLUMBERS GLAZIERS + GASFITTERS

+ James Bennett	14 Westgate
+Joseph Easton	23 Westgate
+George Woollen	Westgate & Masbro Street

ROPE & TWINE MAKERS

James Hattersley	140 Westgate
William Worth	26 Westgate

SHOPKEEPERS

John Clapson	39 Westgate
Charles Copley	57 Westgate
John Dickinson	69 Westgate
William Hallam	72 Westgate
Mary Ann Nadin	61 Westgate
Mary Ann Reynolds	55 Westgate
Amelia Smith	35 Westgate
Ann Turner	138 Westgate
Samuel Wintle	76 Westgate

TAILORS+WOOLLEN DRAPERS

Geo Barnby	16 & 88 Westgate
William Myers	1 Prospect Place Westgate

VETERINARY SURGEONS

John Clapson	39 Westgate

REFERENCES
FRONTISPIECE PHOTOGRAPH
EMILY EDWARDS MARGARET JACKSON

EXTRACTS FROM DRAKES DIRECTORY 1862
OCCUPANTS, TRADES & PROFESSIONS OF WESTGATE

ADVERTISEMENTS
JOSEPH EASTON PLUMBER, GLAZIER & GASFITTER
GEORGE BURRELL BOOT & SHOEMAKER

Two

Chapels

Westgate Baptist Chapel

This photograph was recovered from the East Atlantic (SS Narrung) in 1912

Reproduced by
kind permission
of David Kenyon

THE OLD CHAPEL DOWNS ROW
1706-1880

The Old Chapel, Downs Row 1706-1840

Overlooking Westgate situated at the top of Oil Mill Fold is The Old Chapel Downs Row, founded by Thomas Hollis in 1704 and opened in 1706. This was the first nonconformist chapel in the town.

The chapel held approximately 150 worshippers with services morning and afternoon, the average congregation being 100. The chapel had green-baize pews for the better class families and narrow pews for the ordinary people. In 1793 seat holders paid from 4/- to £5.5.0 per year while many others attended free of pew rent. The Hollis schoolmaster paid 16/-.

The Rev Jacob Brettell (pictured right) was minister of the Old Chapel from 1816-1859. By 1841 the Chapel had become greatly dilapidated. The pews were 'shaky' and the flooring unsound, although it is said the youngsters regarded the holes in the floor as ideal for a game of marbles.

With the help of his congregation Rev Brettell undertook an almost entire rebuilding programme. The cost, originally estimated at £400 soon doubled and he travelled hundreds of miles fund raising.

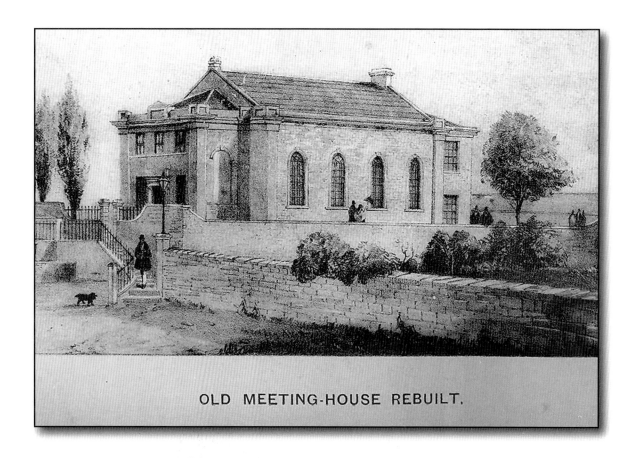

OLD MEETING-HOUSE REBUILT.

The Old Chapel rebuilt 1841

Little was left of the old Chapel, new doorways, windows and a spacious porch were added to the front and a vestry and library to the rear. The main entrance was moved to its present position.

The re-opening of the Chapel took place on Wednesday 11th August 1841. Following the service, congregation and friends adjourned to the Courthouse for 'an excellent repast'. Rev Brettell continued his ministry until 1859 and died in 1862. He is buried in the graveyard surrounding the Chapel.

During the ministry of Rev W Blazeby 1860-1894 he brought about alterations inside the chapel. He introduced an organ replacing 'the stringed band' which consisted of two violins, cello and double bass. The congregation thought the new instrument would never come up the old band.

Rev Blazeby (pictured right) had a vision of a new church and a plot of land was acquired in Moorgate. The foundation stone was laid in 1878 and two years later the Church of Our Father opened.

Sunday the 15th February 1880 saw the last service in The Old Chapel. In later years it became known as the schoolroom and was home to the social activities of the Church, bazaars, plays, youth club, jumble sales etc.

A 1936 'production' in
The Old Chapel

REFERENCE;

The Old Chapel, Downs Row, was referred to as 'Hollis Croft Meeting House' and Hollis Croft Chapel in John Hill's Resume of the Hollis School'.   December 1892.

THE BAPTIST CHAPEL

The Baptist congregation met originally in Clough Road Masborough. On 27th April 1836 the foundation stone of the new chapel was laid in Westgate and the Rev David Charles Clarke of Dronfield officiated. The building had a handsome stone frontage in the classical style and cost approximately £1300. The chapel opened in April 1837 with 26 members, some coming from the church on Masbrough Common. The Rev James Buck was ordained pastor and stayed until his resignation in January 1841.

Sunday School records for September 1850 show that plans were made for the Children's Tea to be held the following year in the open air 'with buns instead of sliced cake'. The treat was arranged for Monday 14th July 1851 at 2 o'clock, scholars to assemble at the Sunday school, proceed into the country and return for tea. Friends may be invited for 1d.

In 1852 teachers were to 'engage heartily in visiting absent scholars' Thomas Dransfield had been a scholar at Westgate Baptist and moved to Masbro' Independant Chapel Sunday school. Being received into Masbro' was contrary to Rotherham & Masbro' Sunday school Union and this was to be pointed out in a letter to them.

One hundred and forty children enjoyed the Sunday school festival held in July 1857 and during the evening the boys played in a field belonging to Mr Bentley. The teachers paid 9d each for tea to increase funds.

Discussion took place in August 1857 regarding the need for an additional schoolroom and a building fund opened. By November this resolution was thought likely to cause division in the church and put on hold.

Plans were made in February 1859 to build a new Sunday school rather than enlarge the original. Recommendations were made to the church to buy a piece of land behind the chapel and a subscription list opened.

'The new school would be warmed by methods other than open fireplaces'.

The following tenders were accepted:

Mason	£183.10.00	Mr Morris
Joiner	£156.10.00	Mr Hawcroft
Painter	£ 6.10.00	Mr Jessop
Plasterer	£ 23.10.00	Mr Gummer
Slater	£ 28.00.00	Mr Heathcote
Plumber	£ 8.18.00	Mr Wooller
Total	**£406.18.00**	

Westgate chapel was improved and the new schoolroom, built at the rear of the chapel cost £1000.00. The first service held there was celebrated on 2nd October 1859.

Westgate Baptist recorded pew rents in its 'Seat Books' 1848-1867 and 1868-1915. Prices varied little from 1868-1915 and some pews are recorded free of rent. The record is divided into 'Bottom' and 'Gallery' and charged according to where one sat.

Rents were paid each quarter- January, April, July and October.

Seats in the 'Bottom' ranged from 1/-, 1/3, 1/6, 2/-, 2/6,

Gallery seats-1/3,1/6.

An example of each is shown below

Bottom 1868	1st quarter	2nd quarter	3rd quarter	4th quarter
Pew no	35			
Sittings each pew	5	5	5	5
Name	Rupert Lomas			
Residence	Westgate			
No of sittings	5	5	5	5
Cost per sitting	2/-	2/-	2/-	2/-
Amt per ¼	10/-	10/-	10/-	10/-
Arrears	5/-	-	-	-
Paid	15/-	10/-	10/-	10/-

Rupert Lomas is recorded as giving up pew 35 in October 1875.

Gallery 1868	1st quarter	2nd quarter	3rd quarter	4th quarter
Pew no	64			
Sittings each pew	3	3	3	3
Name	Chas Steer			
Residence	Westgate			
No of Sittings	2	2	2	1
Cost per sitting	1/6	1/6	1/6	1/3
Amt per ¼	3/-	3/-	3/-	1/3
Arrears	3/-	-	-	-
Paid	6/-	3/-	3/	3/-

During the 4th quarter Chas Steer is allotted 3 sittings per pew but is now only paying for one sitting [1/3]. 1st quarter 1869 Master and Miss Foers join in and pay for 2@1/6 [3/-]. By July 1872 Chas Steer has disappeared and the Foers continue to pay 1/6 each. In 1874 Master Foers is now shown as Herbert Foers and continues to pay for two places.

During 1890, renovation work was carried out both inside and outside the chapel and a porch added to the entrance. A new organ was installed in November 1895.

Several pews were given up around the period 1898-1900.

A small group of members broke away from the chapel in 1901 and met in Alma Road and the Temperance Hall, however, by 1904 the two groups were reunited. The congregation continued to worship in the Baptist Chapel until 1969 when they joined with East Dene Baptist Church and the chapel became the home of the Elim Penticostal Church.

WESTGATE MISSION CHURCH.

Towards the end of the 19th century All Saints Church was making a determined attempt to spread the Christian faith. All Saints looked towards outreach and by 1885 there were mission churches at Ickles, Brinsworth, Catcliffe, Clifton and Westgate.

By 1888 numbers of children attending Sunday school reached 1203 and 110 had volunteered to become teachers. The social life of the church increased with Bazaars, Sewing parties and Friendly Societies.

A new Westgate Mission Church opened in 1885 by Coke Lane near the Baptist Chapel. Prior to this the Parish magazine 'Homewords for Hearth and Home' show Westgate Mission at 54 Westgate in 1883 and in 1884 the Feoffees allowed the use of 20 Westgate before it became a Temperance Hotel. The mission then moved into premises at the top of Burrells buildings, with the work continuing as before.

Weather permitting, Open Air Services were also held in the Courts for people not wishing to go into the Mission Room or Church.

In 1887 Westgate Mission held its first Annual Festival and was congratulated on 'the flourishing conditions of the little school, and the solid result which its work was producing in the manners and morals of the Westgate children'.

The Mission Rooms were a centre not only for Mission Services and Sunday school but also for Mothers Meetings, Boys Clubs and Sewing groups. In 1893 the Band of Hope held their first meeting with 53 members and in 1894 the Church Lads Brigade 'Westgate Mission 'A' Company' had a weekly attendance of over 70.

The Sunday school outing in July 1897 visited Roche Abbey travelling by Waggonettes. After heavy rain on the outward journey a fine afternoon ensued. Following tea a 'scamper' through the woods [and water], and a pleasant ride home brought to an end a day 'so trying to the teaching superintendents'.

In 1905 a church extension scheme was launched with a target of £1900, part of which was to be devoted to the extension of Westgate Mission. Further progress was made to the parish's building programme prior to the First World War and a new Mission Hall opened in Westgate in 1909.

As the war progressed the churchwardens reported a debt of £700 on the Westgate Hall

Plans for The New Westgate Mission Hall opened 1909

During the Second World War, Westgate Hall was taken over by the Corporation as a communal feeding centre. By 1941 a new restaurant was opened in the old Mission Hall able to feed 200 people at one sitting. It was designed to provide a good hot meal as cheaply as possible:

Soup and bread 2d, Meat and two vegetables 6d, Pudding 2d. Children's meal 4d. Cup of tea 1d.

A secondary reason behind the opening of the restaurant was to have in place a method of feeding homeless people in the event of Rotherham being blitzed.

The mission churches at Ickles and Westgate having thrived over the previous fifty years were in decline. By the end of the war, areas of parochial life had been neglected, and this was evident in Westgate and Ickles. Old dwelling houses had given way to industrial development and the area was becoming de-populated.

During the war years Westgate Hall was requisitioned by the Admiralty. Post war it was rented by the Education Committee for £60 per annum. An agreement made to make good any damage done during the war years lasted into the 1960's.

The sale of Westgate Hall to the Post Office for £12,500 was finally concluded in the early 1970's. The site was to be used for a new Telephone Exchange.

THE PRIMITIVE METHODISTS

The Primitive Methodist missionaries began in this area with Camp Meetings held on Ravenfield Common, Mexbro' Common and Silverwood. They were active in Greasbro' and Masbro' in 1819 and Rotherham in 1820. Services were probably held originally in the open air before moving into a room above 35-37 Westgate.

Entrance was gained through the second door and by a winding staircase to the Chapel. The door on the extreme right opened into what was known as 'Ranters Chapel Yard'.

They were known locally as 'The Ranters Chapel'.

John Guest mentions 'Meeting in a humble house of worship in Westgate'

Church and Sunday school became established in the town and the Sunday School Anniversary became a popular event. The journal of Rev T Morgan 1845 indicated that the Westgate chapel became too small for Anniversary occasions and these were celebrated in other premises.

By 1851 a site was secured in Wellgate to provide a chapel, schoolroom and ministers house to accommodate their growing needs. The good work began in Westgate continued.

*35-37 Westgate
The first Primitive Methodist preaching room in Rotherham.*

Handbill for the Temperance Institute Reading Room & Library 1843

REFERENCES

THE OLD CHAPEL DOWNS ROW
BLAZEBY REV W.M. BA ROTHERHAM MEETING HOUSE
& ITS MINISTERS 1906
HILL JOHN RESUME OF THE HOLLIS SCHOOL 1892-
REF HOLLIS CROFT CHAPEL
HOLLIS TRUST

THE BAPTIST CHAPEL WESTGATE
GUEST JOHN HISTORIC NOTICES OF ROTHERHAM 1879
DRAKES DIRECTORY 1862
WHITES DIRECTORY 1901
ROTHERHAM ADVERTISER 26/11/1859 PGE 4, 17/05/1890
PGE2,
ROTHERHAM ARCHIVE LIST 2 REF 131/N
SUNDAY SCHOOL MINUTE BOOK 1849-1862
WESTGATE BAPTIST SEAT BOOK RECORDS 1848-1867,
1868-1915

WESTGATE MISSION CHURCH
OAKLEY WLLIAM YE OLDE ROTHERHAM TOWN 1915
CATER PHYLLIS M SO GREAT A CLOUD OF WITNESSES
1983
THE ROTHERHAM ADVERTISER 25TH JANUARY 1941 &
28TH JUNE 1972
ROTHERHAM PARISH MAGAZINES 'HOMEWORDS FOR
HEARTH & HOME'
1884-1903.

PRIMITIVE METHODISTS
GUEST JOHN HISTORIC NOTICES OF ROTHERHAM 1879
page 483.
METHODIST PRESS CUTTINGS JUNE 1920 ROTHERHAM
ARCHIVES
SOUVENIR PROGRAMME OF GRAND RAINBOW BAZAAR
1913- ROTHERHAM ARCHIVES   REF 367-N/30/1/1

PHOTOGRAPHS
THE ORIGINAL OLD CHAPEL 1706 & CHAPEL REBUILT
1841, REV J BRETTELL, REV W BLAZEBY
ROTHERHAM OLD MEETING HOUSE & ITS MINISTERS
BY W BLAZEBY BA 1906
1936 'PRODUCTION' OLD CHAPEL
MARGARET JACKSON

ROTHERHAM ARCHIVES & LOCAL STUDY SERVICE
WESTGATE MISSION 1909 - PLANS
35-37 WESTGATE SOUVENIR PROGRAMME OF GRAND
RAINBOW BAZAAR 1913
HANDBILL FOR THE TEMPERANCE INSTITUTE 1843

WESTGATE BAPTIST CHAPEL PH SLATER OF
HILLSBOROUGH

WESTGATE BAPTIST CHAPEL (frontispiece Chapter 2)
DAVID KENYON - PIANO CENTRE

JAMES SIMMONS BIBLE 1892 WIN MAPPLEBECK
WESTGATE RESTAURANT ROTHERHAM ADVERTISER
25TH JANUARY 1941

Three

Schools

The *Hollis School 1890 Oil Mill Fold*

THE HOLLIS SCHOOL

The Hollis School was founded in 1702 by Thomas Hollis the elder for the education of poor children of Rotherham.

In 1789 the school was rebuilt and situated in Oil Mill Fold opposite the Old Chapel.

John Hill's 'Resume of the History of the Hollis School' stated the school was further endowed by contributions from the trustees and other protestant dissenters and referred to this endowment as The Hollis Croft 'Rimingtons' property, formally the old 'Horse Oil Mill', which consisted of 11 cottages and land upon which the school was built. Two of the cottages were sited above the school and occupied by the schoolmaster and mistress.

Thomas Hollis thought that education and religious training should go hand in hand and the schoolmaster received £20 per year for teaching 20-30 poor children free.

The school consisted of a one-storey building of red sandstone with a slate roof. The single large room was divided by a wooden partition which when taken to pieces formed a number of long tea tables.

The mistress of the girls was Miss Ramsbottom who was well liked and gave the girls a useful knowledge of sewing and knitting. The schoolmaster Henry Taylor, an excellent violinist used the cane with some success in educating his scholars.

Miss Ramsbottom eventually retired to the comfort of one of the almshouses and 'fiddler Henry' found another more congenial occupation.

The rules of the school were as follows:

1] Children should attend regularly in as decent apparel as possible and any child absent for more than 13 days would be excluded.

2] Children should attend Sunday school and public worship morning and afternoon, any child missing for more than three 'Sabbeths' to be excluded.

3] The design of this institution—To train a child in the way he should go.

4] To pay attention to the moral conduct of children out of school hours.

Any child found lying, swearing, pilfering or playing about in the streets or fields on the Lords day would be chastised.

The Hollis School under Mr Joseph Ramsbottom had a most unpromising pupil called Ebenezer Elliott of whom he could make nothing and finally gave him up in despair. Ebenezer went to Thurlstone to live with relatives for a year and then returned to the Hollis School. In later life Elliott was to pay tribute to the schoolmaster.

The minister of the Chapel, inspired by educational reform, decided to improve Hollis School in 1862 by adding an upper room. This was reached by a winding staircase constructed in a tower to the front of the building serving as an entrance for both boys and girls.

The school became a public elementary school upon the passing of the Elementary Education Act 1870. It is said to have done for the poor classes of Rotherham what the Grammar school did for the richer class.

In 1884 the average attendance was boys 57 and girls 61. Later the two departments held 144 pupils. In 1893 the trustees let the school building to the Rotherham schools board at a yearly rent of £35. They took over the school as it was. No change was made to teachers or children.

The school continued until 1896 when the local education authority constructed further school buildings of its own.

After closure the Hollis School was converted into three cottages and together with two other cottages formally used by the teachers were rented out.

A tablet erected over the front of the school read

In the year 1702

A school for the education of poor children

In Rotherham was endowed by Thomas Hollis Snr.

Of London, and afterwards his descendants.

And in 1789

This building was erected. And the school further endowed

For the same purpose by the contribution of several

Of the trustees and other Protestant dissenters.

The upper room, turret and other parts were added in 1862

By like voluntary efforts to the above.

For information

In 1996 during renovations to the outside of The Old Chapel and surrounding graveyard, a new stone tablet was erected on the side of the building to commemorate the Hollis School replacing the original which was illegible.

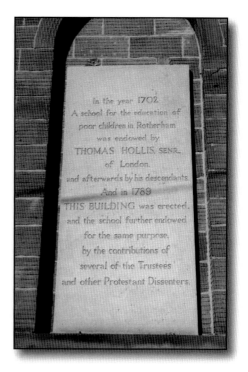

THE HOLLIS SCHOOL LOG BOOK OCTOBER 1874-JULY 1896.

The Hollis school Log book recorded children's school life over a period of twenty years. H M Inspectors frequently visited the school and pupils were regularly tested on their subjects.

October 6th 1874

The school remained open during the 'Statutes Week' [a holiday week in town] with much diminished numbers of scholars in attendance.

November 5th 1874.

A letter sent to Rev W Blazeby [on behalf of managers of the Hollis School] enclosed a report made by H M Inspector giving examination results.
Total of pupils presented 72
Passed on examination - Reading 62, Writing 43, Arithmetic 33

September 1875

Total of pupils presented 76
Passed on examination - Reading 76, Writing 75, Arithmetic 66
Gross total of grant claimed £86.12.0

September 30th 1878

The numbers of pupils had risen to 117. No grant was payable although the results were good because the school had infringed Article 17. The school had accommodation for a maximum of 72 children and average attendance had increased to 124.

October 1880

The Annual report of the Boys School:
Considering the crowded state of the room, the school was in 'very fair order'. Geography and Grammar had reached the required level and the standard in general was very satisfactory. Reading was clear and distinct but occasionally too loud.

December 5th 1884

A Snowstorm caused many children to stay away from school. Those in attendance were taught their first song, 'Catch the Sunshine'. More songs followed and by March 1885 a dozen boys were taught to sing 'seconds' to the Lords Prayer.

June 26th 1885

Very low attendance because the boys visited Wentworth Park to see the Volunteer Review.

May 1886

Attendance was irregular due to 'rough weather'. Drill was omitted and the school closed Friday afternoon on account of the floods.

February 1891

A visit from the sub inspector found the boys and girls playing together in the girls yard without supervision. The headmaster was asked to explain!

August 1891

The Managers of the school authorised the following fees to be charged from 1st September 1891. Standard classes – I, II, III, one penny per week - IV, twopence per week - V, VI, VII threepence per week

18th December 1891

John Croft was again punished for playing truant and at the request of his father he received a crust of bread and was locked in during dinnertime. John Croft clearly did not like school as his name appeared frequently for missed lessons and playing truant.

September 1893

Different passages of the bible were read to the pupils. During the week of 15th September 1893, 31 boys received free breakfasts one morning and 36 another having a beneficial effect on attendance. By 24th November1893 these were discontinued.

November 1893

The boys managed reasonably well but overcrowding made teaching difficult. Reading was fluent and accurate but more care was needed in writing and composition. Spelling needed attention as did Arithmetic in some standards.

May 1895

Merit or Reward cards given out for good attendance.

September 1895

Many children were late or absent as they watched 'the conveyances passing through the town to the Doncaster Races'.

One of the last reports of the Hollis School said that the boys were 'in good order' considering the difficulties under which the work was carried out and their attainments were creditable.

No further grants would be paid to the school in its present premises. The School finally closed on 16th July 1896 and all 'apparatus' was moved to the new school.

The scholars, Headmaster and teacher Wilfred Green were transferred to Alma Road School which opened after the midsummer holiday on 10th August 1896.

WESTGATE CHAPEL TEMPORARY BOARD SCHOOL 1893-1896

The school opened 13th February 1893 with 44 girls and 20 infants. Miss Ruth Gilbody a certificated teacher led the staff.

17th February 1893

The total registered number of pupils was 126 and later increased to 150 per week. There was a list of 'Object Lessons' for the infants under the headings Animal Life, Vegetable Life, Common Objects and Natural Phenomena.

2nd March 1893

Several girls attended irregularly and had not been to school since The Ickles School had closed the previous October.

24th March 1893

The infant room was now full.

7th July 1893

The children enjoyed a day's holiday to celebrate the Royal Wedding.

15th September 1893

Over a two-day period 124 breakfasts were given to children whose parents were out of work.

26th October 1893.

Her Majesty's Inspector of Schools visited the Girls school and gave an excellent report praising the teachers who achieved such good results in so short a time. 'Needlework was carefully taught and recitations well said but more attention was needed in Arithmetic'. Similar praise was received for the infants.

3rd November 1893.

Several children were absent from school because they had no shoes to wear. Breakfasts were continued for the children during the holiday period although the school was closed for Statutes week.

17th November 1893.

Many children away from school either sick or for lack of clothing.

20th July 1894

A list of youths names were given to the Superintendent of Police for constantly annoying the teachers by throwing stones at the school door.

7th September 1894

The teachers were having difficulty with the attendance of a number of children. The parents kept them at home and ignored the warning notices from the Board.

19th October 1894

The boys were transferred to The Feoffees School and the girls put into Standard class 1. By the end of November the attainment of the girls school was highly satisfactory. The Infants class was also praised despite the work being carried on in a temporary room ill adapted for teaching purposes.

21st December 1894.

One of the teachers, Miss Hutchinson left to go to St Ann's school. In February 1895 the Board decided not to replace her and instead transferred Standard classes 4 & 5, eighteen girls in total to Wellgate School.

19th July 1895

Fifty children were away from school at the 'Baptist Treat'. The following Friday the school closed for the summer vacation and re-opened three weeks later12th August 1895.

25th October 1895

Twenty four girls were transferred to Wellgate Board school and fourteen infant boys to The Feoffees Board school.

6th November 1895

HM Inspectors visited again and reported that the infants must not exceed 43 in number as long as the school remained in temporary premises. They also wished to know whether the Board could state a date for the children to be transferred to a permanent building and the temporary school closed.

13th December 1895

Miss Gilbody left the school to become mistress of Wellgate Board School.

Westgate Chapel Temporary Board School finally closed 16th July 1896 and after the three weeks summer holiday pupils were transferred to the new schools in Alma Road.

THE ROTHERHAM WESLEYAN SCHOOL

is recorded in Slaters Directory 1887 as being on Wilfred Street. The school was built in the chapel yard of the original Octagon Chapel and stood on the site of the old Labour Exchange.

The Headmaster of the School about 1865 was Mr Joseph Cox, father of John Crowther Cox who was widely known as a photographer but more locally as part of the auctioneering firm Cox, Dewar & Beaton.

The Infants Log Book 1863-1892 commenced on Monday 2nd February 1863 with an HMI Inspection of the school reporting the number of pupils totalled 144 and were clean and neat in appearance.

The children were classified according to age into Sections A, B & C.

Section B was supplied with reading books at 1d each to use 3 times per week in place of the large reading sheet usually used.

March 1863 Number of pupils had risen to 168. A marching lesson had been included in the curriculum with new flags.

9th March 1863 There was little work done and much excitement in anticipation of the following day.

10th March 1863 Marriage of The Prince of Wales and Princess Alexandra of Denmark. The children formed part of the procession through town and everyone enjoyed a Gala Day.

After the summer holidays 100 children recommenced at the school which was given a good report for being a well equipped school and well taught. The work was rewarded with 'an active joyous spirit, unusual singing and excellent manual exercises.'

*27th April 1864 The children were taken for an afternoon in a field at Moorgate which had been loaned for the occasion.

1875 The infants were reported as being fairly intelligent and carefully taught.

By 1886 it was thought that suitable desks should be provided for writing. 'The gallery in the babies room should be supplied with tables or shelves and the back rails lowered to support the loins instead of chafing the shoulders'. There was much sickness in school due to Whooping Cough.

The list of lessons to be given to the infants was, Natural History, Common Objects, Natural Phenomina, Form and Colour and Moral Conversational Lessons eg;

1] Domestic Animals   Goat, Fowl, Fox

2] Foreign Animals   Eagle, Crocodile, Kangaroo

3] Common Objects   The Carrot, Cherries, Baskets

4] Natural Phenomina   Day & Night, The Moon, Rain.

5] Conversational   Coins, The Sea, The Seasons

6] Moral   The Shepherds Boy, The Lion & The Mouse,

7] Form   Straight & Curved Lines, Building with Cubes

8] Colour   Naming Colours, Primary Colours

Songs prepared for the Annual Inspection were;

The Cooper, The Cat & the Kittens, The Drummer Boy and The Mill Wheels are Clapping.

Recitations prepared were

Ba Ba Black Sheep, The Sick Doll and The Blind Boy.

The Inspection of 1890 remarked that the general efficiency of the infants department was below the level required and stated that 'Unless the managers were prepared to supply skilled teachers they would be better to discontinue the use of the grimy gloomy room'. 'The premises were ill adapted and they were in a dingy and depressing environment'

*Gummer remarked that the Wilfred Street school playground was 'uneven and quite unsuitable'. The children used the fields of Moorgate as a playground in the area of the Church Of Our Father, Douglas Street and Stanley Street.

The log is recorded until 1892 although the school must have continued longer as pupils are shown transferring into Hollis School as late as November 1895.

OTHER SCHOOLS

Drakes Directory 1862 records a teaching academy at 81 Westgate run by Martha Barton and Gummer mentions that nearby to John Clarke, Land Agent and Accountant, resided his daughters who conducted a school for young ladies which was well attended.

'There were several good academies in the town, one run in Westgate by the Misses Clarke'.

REFERENCE
BLAZEBY REV WILLIAM BA THE HOLLIS SCHOOL ROTHERHAM OLD MEETING HOUSE & ITS MINISTERS 1906
HILL JOHN RESUME OF THE HOLLIS SCHOOL 1892 HOLLIS TRUST

ARCHIVES & LOCAL STUDY SERVICE ROTHERHAM
THE HOLLIS SCHOOL LOG BOOK 1874-1896
WESTGATE TEMPORARY BOARD SCHOOL LOG BOOK 1893-1896
ROTHERHAM WESLEYAN SCHOOL LOG BOOK 1863-1892
GUMMER GEORGE REMINISCENCES OF ROTHERHAM 1927
GUEST JOHN HISTORIC NOTICES OF ROTHERHAM 1879

ROTHERHAM ADVERTISER 25/11/2005

ILLUSTRATION
THE HOLLIS SCHOOL 1890 – POSTCARD M JACKSON

OTHER SCHOOLS
DRAKES DIRECTORY 1862

GUMMER GEORGE REMINISCENCES OF ROTHERHAM 1927

Four

Industry

**FOUNDRIES
BY THE RIVER DON
WESTGATE**

REF 7080   *Circa 1860-1867*

Looking North East from Bow Bridge with the Wheathill Foundry on the right bank and Guest &
Chrimes to the left. A Yorkshire keel is moored on the River Don near to its confluence with the
River Rother.

FOUNDRIES

Rotherham had an established industry of Ironfounding during the nineteenth century and several foundries were situated along the banks of the River Don at Westgate. This proximity allowed transportation of goods to the rest of Britain by waterway and the commencement of the Railway in Rotherham from 1838 also allowed a growth of the Stove Grate industry.

In 1850 approximately 365 people were employed in casting and forging and 350 in the stove grate works. In 1860 Rotherham claimed to be the centre of the stove grate industry and its products pronounced among the best in the country.

BATHS FOUNDRY

REF 00129   *Baths Foundry Westgate circa 1881-1900*

Ref 01596

George Aizlewood opened the Baths Foundry on the site of the old privately owned public baths in Westgate.

By 1849 the proprietor was William Aizlewood and in 1852 the firm was listed as Aizlewood & Co. During 1854 Joseph Aizlewood took over the Baths Foundry and by 1856 it was again known as Aizlewood & Co.

Henry Tomlinson, a grocer from Masbro' was the next proprietor taking over in 1860. He showed an example of his invention of the 'Patent Pneumatic Movable Fire Grate' at the 1862 International Exibition.

Following the retirement of Henry Tomlinson in 1865, Messrs Morgan, Macaulay and Waide took over ownership of the Baths foundry. The new firm held a supper at the Crown Hotel for 90 workmen and friends in honour of the retirement and in celebration of the new company. They continued until 1872 and their successors Morgan & Waide renamed the foundry, Baths Works, continuing until 1883 when they ceased the manufacture of stove grates.

In September 1887 a serious fire broke out at the premises of the Baths foundry. The buildings were situated in the midst of a densely populated area and this caused great alarm. The upper floor was stocked with stoves, baths, and castings in all stages of manufacture and the ground floor was divided between a workshop and a warehouse. Other surrounding work-shops employed around 100 men.

The fire was first noticed by Charles Johnson of Burrells Row who saw 'an unusual light through his window and raised the alarm'. The fire took approximately four hours to extinguish and fortunately the fire brigade managed to contain the fire within the building in which it had first started. Damage was estimated at around £1000.

The Rotherham Advertiser account of the fire stated 'It is pleasing to note that the workmen will not be thrown idle and operations will be resumed as usual on Monday'.

In October 1892 another fire was to damage the Baths foundry. This started in the bath enamelling shop and was thought to be due to the overheating of the enamelling stove. The estimated cost this time was between £200-£300.

The Rotherham Steel Strip Co Ltd bought the Baths Foundry which had been standing idle for many years and installed a cold rolling mill. Work commenced January 1917.

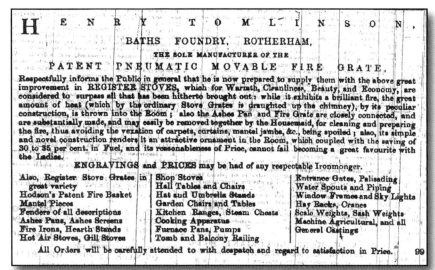

WHEATHILL FOUNDRY

Wheathill Foundry Westgate circ 1891-1900

The Wheathill foundry was established by Joseph Aizlewood to make stove grates and by 1854 he had joined in partnership with Jackson & Redmayne. During 1854 Joseph Aizlewood left to manage the Baths foundry.

Messrs Watson, Redmayne & Co manufactured stove grates at the Wheathill foundry until 1860 when Thomas Redmayne & Co took over. Between 1861-1862 the company was known as Redmayne & Co.

In 1863 The Wheathill foundry was leased by William Owen to accommodate his increasing business. He was born near the Baptist chapel in Westgate, the son of a maltster. William was apprenticed to the pattern making business and continued a successful career at the Phoenix foundry in partnership with Charles Sandford.

William Owen was the patentee of several inventions for making solid wrought iron wheels and tyres. In 1864 he formed a Limited company, Owens Patent Wheel, Tire and Axle Co Ltd and operated from the Phoenix works until going into liquidation in 1872. Owen retained the stove grate kitchen range and general casting business, operating from the Wheathill foundry where he remained until his death in 1881.

The Wheathill Foundry Co Ltd continued until 1888 when it was taken over by Thomas Watson [& Sons], whose father ran the foundry between 1854 -1860.

During February 1893 the National Union of Stove Grate Workers held a mass meeting of workmen in Rotherham. The men of Wheathill foundry had been given fourteen days notice to leave their employment. Mr Sanders stated that the men of the Wheathill foundry were true to their motto 'Shoulder to Shoulder'. The Wheathill foundry was the oldest in the town in respect of its kitchen range dating back to the Walker family.

At an extraordinary meeting of the shareholders of Thomas Watson & Sons held at the Royal Victoria Hotel Sheffield in February 1893 a decision was made to wind up the company.

The Wheathill foundry returned to stove grate manufacture when George Wright [Rotherham] Ltd moved there in 1953/4.

HARRIS'S FOUNDRY

REF 15686   *Harris's Foundry Westgate circa 1860-1870*

Jarvis Harris established Westgate foundry in the 1820's and was said to be 'a hard working and ingenious man'. He is listed in Whites directory of 1841 as being on Westgate and Wellgate. By 1856 the firm was under the name of Harris Robert & Jarvis, Stove Grate Makers at the Westgate foundry. An 1860 directory records Robert Harris & Jarvis on Sheffield Road and from 1861-1868 the firm was known as R&J Harris Stove Grate Makers. The business continued as a light castings foundry into the 20th century.

Harris's foundry produced some of the largest castings in the district. It was a common site to see these being conveyed on low trucks drawn sometimes by 'eight and ten horses to their destination'. Orders of huge castings weighing from 40-60 tons were undertaken by the firm. R&J Harris became famous for producing the heaviest castings for the enormous Anvil Blocks required for iron plate manufacture and railway wheels.

Jarvis Harris was also a member of the town council after the incorporation of the borough and served 1871-1874.

The Rotherham Advertiser 30th July 1892 recorded the death of Jarvis Harris and stated that he was a partner in the firm R&J Harris until approximately 1882.

Harris's remained at Westgate foundry until 1900 and was succeeded by George Cawwood.

R. & J. HARRIS,

ROTHERHAM.

IRON AND BRASS

FOUNDERS,

MANUFACTURERS OF STOVE GRATES

And all kinds of Heavy Castings.

CHILLED ROLLS OF ALL KINDS.

RAILWAY FOUNDRY

GEORGE NEATBY,

Ironfounder, and Manufacturer of Stove Grates and Kitchen Ranges,

ENGINEERS' AND MILLWRIGHTS' WORK, &c.,

RAILWAY FOUNDRY,

George Neatby is shown on the 1851 census as being 33 years old and an Ironmoulder. He lived at 27 Oil Mill Fold with his wife Hannah aged 34 and their 3 children, William aged 12, James aged 5 and Benjamin aged 2.

In February 1854 the Hollis Trustees leased a piece of land situated on the west side of Westgate, containing 925 square yards together with several messuages or tenements and buildings to George Neatby by Indenture of Lease from 25th March for a term of 99 years. This was subject to a yearly rent of £18.

The Indenture itself described a piece or parcel of ground on the West side of Westgate abutting towards the East on Westgate and towards the West and North on land and tenements of John Nightingale and towards the South on land and tenements of Joseph Aizlewood. The rent was to be paid in equal portions 25th March & 29th September.

[This land was sold to Rotherham Corporation in 1909].

The 1861 census shows George Neatby and family living at 27 Westgate.

Drakes Directory 1862 lists George Neatby as an Iron & Brassfounder & Stove Grate Manufacturer at the Railway Foundry and also a Beerhouse keeper at 27 Westgate

Other directories list Neatby as, a Moulder and Beer Retailer at 27 Westgate in 1859, an Ironfounder and Beerhouse keeper of 27 Westgate in 1861 and in 1864 he is listed as an Ironfounder and Manufacturer of Stove Grates, Engineers and Millwrights work—Railway Foundry Westgate.

He is also recorded as Licensee of The Alma Tavern 1860-1869 at 25 Westgate although he died 5th March 1868.

His wife Hannah is listed in an 1871 Directory as Ironfounder and Beerhouse keeper at 27 Westgate. She is also recorded as Licensee of The Alma Tavern following on from her husband 1870-1899. Hannah died 23rd June 1899 aged 82 years.

Westgate Miscellaneous Industries

NAILMAKING

The factory of William Favell in Oil Mill Fold claimed to be the largest in the horse nail trade. The proprietor, a well-known solicitor had as manager Mr Ben Moss and eventually the business became his property.

Mr Hadfield, whose work was connected with the railways spoke of his memories of Rotherham upon his retirement in 1908, and recorded that he had 'seen men coming from the surrounding districts to be supplied with bundles of rods, which they took home to manufacture into nails at their little smithies'. They returned with the nails and were paid for their labour. Machinery subsequently replaced the handmade article.

Dickinson's Nails were also well known, their factory being in Westgate until it moved to larger premises in Drummond Street.

BRASS INDUSTRY

PAYNE BROTHERS,
WESTGATE, ROTHERHAM,
MANUFACTURERS OF ALL KINDS OF
PLUMBERS' BRASS WORK.
Mill and Engine Brasses cast on reasonable terms, and on the shortest notice.

James Payne owned a small factory in Water Lane, Westgate and was the first maker of water taps.

REFERENCE

FOUNDRIES WESTGATE

BATHS FOUNDRY-
MORLEY CHRIS THE STOVE GRATE RANGE & DECORATIVE CAST IRON INDUSTRY OF ROTHERHAM CHAPTER 11 ASPECTS OF ROTHERHAM 3 1998
ROTHERHAM ADVERTISER- 19/04/1862, / 18/03/1865, / 10/09/1887, / 29/10/1892

WHEATHILL FOUNDRY-
MORLEY CHRIS CHAPTER 11 ASPECTS OF ROTHERHAM 3 1998
GUEST JOHN HISTORIC NOTICES OF ROTHERHAM 1879
DRAKES DIRECTORY 1862,
ROTHERHAM ADVERTISER 22/01/1881, 11/02/1893.

HARRIS'S FOUNDRY-
MORLEY CHRIS CHAPTER 11 ASPECTS OF ROTHERHAM 3 1998
GUEST JOHN HISTORIC NOTICES OF ROTHERHAM 1879
GUESTS RELICS & RECORDS VOL 3 [GREEN]
GUMMER G REMINISCENCES OF ROTHERHAM 1927
ROTHERHAM ADVERTISER 30/07/1892 PGE5

RAILWAY FOUNDRY-
CHRIS MORLEY CHAPTER 11 ASPECTS OF ROTHERHAM 3 1998
HOLLIS TRUST CHARITY COMMISSIONERS DOCUMENT 1884
INDENTURE COPY 15TH FEBRUARY 1854
DRAKES DIRECTORY 1862

PHOTOGRAPHS
ROTHERHAM ARCHIVES & LOCAL STUDY SERVICE
WHEATHILL FOUNDRY/GUEST & CHRIMES REF 7080 PHOTOGRAPHER UNKNOWN
BATHS FOUNDRY WESTGATE-1881-1900 REF 00129 PHOTOGRPHER UNKNOWN
HENRY TOMLINSON 1865-1875 REF 01596 CROSBY, J LEADBEATER, JAMES
WHEATHILL FOUNDRY 1891-1900 REF 00124 PHOTOGRAPHER UNKNOWN
HARRIS'S FOUNDRY 1860-1870 REF 15686.PHOTOGRAPHER UNKNOWN

ADVERTISEMENTS
DRAKES DIRECTORY 1862
GEORGE NEATBY RAILWAY FOUNDRY
R & J HARRIS IRON & BRASS FOUNDERS

HENRY TOMLINSON BATHS FOUNDRY- ROTHERHAM ADVERTISER 25/04/1863

MISCELLANEOUS INDUSTRIES
NAILMAKING
GUMMER G REMINISCENCES OF ROTHERHAM 1927
ROTHERHAM ADVERTISER 1/02/1908

BRASS INDUSTRY
GUMMERS REMINISCENCES OF ROTHERHAM 1927
ADVERTISEMENT
DRAKES DIRECTORY 1862 [PAYNE BROTHERS]

FIVE

Transport

REF 06637   *Westgate Railway Station Bridge 1858-1867*

REF 10368   *Sheffield & Rotherham Railway 1838 Commemorative Mug*

CRITERION.

THE Public are respectfully informed, that for their better accommodation, an Elegant New OMNIBUS has commenced running from the PALACE INN, Bakers' Hill, Sheffield, to Rotherham and back, carrying Twelve Passengers inside, which for comfort and accommodation cannot be excelled, it being the determination of the Proprietors, to work it in a style superior to anything yet brought before the *Inhabitants of Sheffield*; and they trust, that a single trial will fully convince them that a conveyance like the CRITERION, has long been very much wanted in Sheffield.

The CRITERION will leave the Palace Inn, punctually every *Sunday Afternoon for Rotherham, at Two o'Clock,* and every Monday, Tuesday, Wednesday, Thursday, and Friday Mornings, at NINE o'Clock, and Afternoons, at Two o'Clock; and every Saturday Morning for DONCASTER, at a Quarter Past Seven o'Clock.

P. S.—The CRITERION will leave Rotherham for Sheffield, on the above-mentioned Mornings, at Eleven, and Afternoons at Five o'Clock.

Performed by
THOMAS CLIFFORD,
SAMUEL BARNETT & CO.

Westgate was one of the main transportation routes in Rotherham. In the late 18th century 'A Genteel Light Coach' was advertised which ran from Sheffield via Rotherham and Doncaster to Hull.

At the end of the Napoleonic wars in 1815 The Walkers obtained a contract to build a cast iron bridge at Southwark. Thousands of people flocked to see the bridge parts displayed in a field near their ironworks. To meet demand a new type of vehicle appeared on the road. These were known as Waterloos [named after the battle], a light high-wheeled vehicle pulled by a horse and described as a 'common sort of jaunting car'. Once the bridge sections were removed to London by canal, the Waterloos were switched to run between Rotherham and Sheffield until the Sheffield and Rotherham Railway opened in 1838. They afforded passengers a cheap though not very elegant form of transport.

Several coaches passed through Rotherham and in 1834 an omnibus named 'The Criterion' ran from Sheffield to Rotherham and back carrying twelve passengers.

Immediately there was competition from another company who put a carriage called 'The Sun' into operation, timed to leave Rotherham at a quarter of an hour prior to The Criterion. 'The Sun' left Mr Babbs at the Pack Horse Inn, Doncaster Gate travelling to the Cross Daggers at the top of High Street, The Wellington Inn, the Swan in Westgate and onto Sheffield.

SHEFFIELD & ROTHERHAM.

THE Gentry and Public are most respectfully informed, that a new light and easy running CARRIAGE, called THE SUN, will commence Running on MONDAY next, the 27th Oct., between SHEFFIELD and ROTHERHAM, Twice a Day. The SUN will leave Mr. BINNS', the Rising Sun, Sheffield Moor, at a quarter before Nine o'Clock every Morning, (Mondays excepted,) and a Quarter before Two every Afternoon; Mr. CLIFTON's, Spread Eagle, High Street, Ten Minutes before Nine in the Morning, and Ten Minutes before Two in the Afternoon; and PERCIVAL's Office, and the BULL and MOUTH, Waingate, at Nine o'Clock in the Morning, and Two o'Clock in the Afternoon. On Monday Mornings, for the Convenience of Passengers to the Rotherham Market, the SUN will leave Sheffield AN HOUR EARLIER.

In returning from Rotherham, the SUN will leave Mr. BABBS, the Pack Horse, a Quarter before Eleven in the Morning, and a Quarter before Five in the Afternoon; Cross Daggers, Wellington Inn, and the Swan, at Eleven o'Clock in the Morning, and Five o'Clock in the Afternoon of every Day.

Performed by the Public's most obedient Servants.
PERCIVAL, BINNS, & CO.

The RED ROVER COACH, to Hull, every Morning, (Sunday excepted,) at Five o'Clock, through Rotherham, Doncaster, Hatfield, and Thorne; from Mr. HOPKINSON's, the Falcon Inn, and Mr. PERCIVAL's Office, Waingate.

D. HOPKINSON and T. PERCIVAL beg to inform their Friends and the Public, that the RED ROVER has no connexion with any other Coaching Establishment. D. HOPKINSON, Coachman.

The ECLIPSE, to Doncaster, every Morning, at Ten o'Clock, and returns at Half past Three.

A MARKET COACH TO DONCASTER, every Saturday Morning, at Half past Seven.
PERCIVAL & CO.

The proposal in 1834 to build a railway was greeted with opposition. There was 'much head shaking around the tea tables in Westgate and High Street' and discussion in workshops, The Crown Hotel and Angel where ' silk hatted sedate old gentlemen and young men in drab pantaloons, blue jackets and silver buttons discussed the project over good brown ale'. It was felt the railroad might encourage the 'more rowdy element among Sheffield people travelling to Rotherham, to upset the peace'.

The estimated cost of the railway was £50,000 and presumed income £7650 per week.

By late 1836 passengers on coaches were able to see 'flags' in the adjacent fields marking out the route of the Sheffield and Rotherham Railway. These were the final years of the coaching age and operated until the railways were built, in some cases bridging the gaps where the railways had not yet reached.

In his journal 'Ye Olde Rotherham Town', William Oakley wrote the following;

'In the coaching days as they run from Rotherham and Sheffield to London one driver of the coaches were Old Rattling Jack. Cracked his whip and off they went. When the coaches run through our town they were the good old days'.

After the opening of the Sheffield and Rotherham Railway new buses and coaches were introduced which met trains at Westgate station and later Masbrough station.

A proprietor named Bletcher began an omnibus service from Westgate to Doncaster. His 1838 advertisement was headed 'Expeditious travelling by Railway and Omnibus to Doncaster every day'.

EXPEDITIOUS TRAVELLING BY RAILWAY AND OMNIBUS TO DONCASTER EVERY DAY.

FRANCIS BLETCHER respectfully informs his Friends and the Public, that he has commenced running an elegant and commodious OMNIBUS EVERY DAY from ROTHERHAM to the White Bear, DONCASTER, taking up the Passengers arriving by the 10 o'Clock Train, and returning in time for the 5 o'Clock Train. On Saturday Mornings, the hour of starting will be on the arrival of the 8 o'Clock Train.

Money Orders are issued and paid at the General Office, and also at the Branch Office, College-road, Masbro' from 9 a.m. to 6 p.m.

RAILWAY CONVEYANCE.

SHEFFIELD AND ROTHERHAM RAILWAY; Station, Westgate—Trains to the Holmes, Brightside and Sheffield eight times a day, and three on Sundays; Henry Turner, station master, Rotherham, and William Simpson at the Holmes

MIDLAND RAILWAY; Station, Masbro'—Trains to Derby and Leeds about nine times on week days, and five on Sundays. To Doncaster four on week days and two on Sundays; and to Sheffield thirteen on week days and seven on Sundays; Thomas Turner, station master.

OMNIBUSES, from the Crown Inn, meet the trains to and from

COACHES AND OMNIBUSES.

To *Bawtry* and *Tickhill*, John Lumley's omnibus from the Pack Horse, and Rotherham and Masbro' Stations every Monday, Tuesday, Thursday, and Saturday at 3.15 p.m.

To *Rawmarsh*, J. Walton and Co.'s omnibus, from the College Inn, several times a day.

CARRIERS BY RAILWAY.

Midland Railway Company, Masbro' Station, to Derby, Leeds, London, and all parts; Thomas Turner, station master.

Hunt and Co., Princess-street, Masbro'; Richard Skidmore, agent.

Pickford and Co., Princess-street, Masbro' to all parts; William Jackson, agent.

Sheffield and Rotherham Railway, Westgate, to Sheffield, &c.; Henry Turner, station master.

South Yorkshire Railway and River Don Co., the Wharf, to Sheffield, Doncaster, Barnsley, and all parts; Joseph Wharam, agent.

CARRIERS.

To Sheffield, George Parkin, from Westgate, daily, except Monday,

WATER CONVEYANCE.

Trading Vessels, between Sheffield, Thorne, Hull, &c., call here to receive and deliver cargoes at the River Don Company's Wharf.

Extract from Drakes Directory 1862

Sheffield & Rotherham Railway Coat of Arms

The Sheffield & Rotherham Railway opened in October 1838 running from Westgate, Rotherham to the Wicker in Sheffield.

Pioneering railway engineer, Isaac Dodds was persuaded by John Stephenson, railway contractor, to oversee the construction of the Sheffield & Rotherham Railway.

Dodds established a locomotive manufacturing plant alongside the line at Holmes and was responsible for constructing a locomotive known as the Cutler, a 2-2-2 engine which gave over 25 years service to the railway.

The line was five miles long, with a branch line to the canal at Greasbrough being added in 1839. In 1845 the Sheffield and Rotherham Railway amalgamated with the Midland Railway.

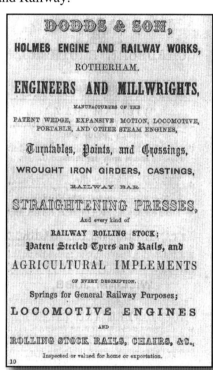

There was great excitement on the morning of the 31st October 1838 when crowds lined the route from Sheffield to Rotherham at every vantage point. The first train to Rotherham was due to leave Sheffield at 10am and the second at 12pm, however, the guest of honour, the Earl Fitzwilliam and his party arrived nearly an hour late. The train eventually left Sheffield station to strains of 'God Save the Queen'. Bands played in Rotherham and Sheffield and church bells rang out all day in both towns.

REF 06649

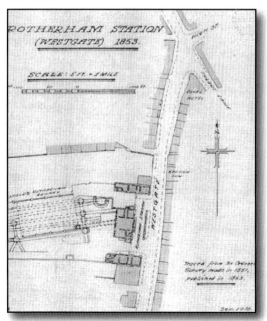

The train arrived at Westgate station at ten past eleven to be greeted by the Rotherham Band who led the procession including the Earls party, to the Court House for a 'sumptuous breakfast' provided at the expense of the Sheffield and Rotherham Railway.

Trains departed from each terminus Westgate and the Wicker every hour during the day. The distance of five miles was covered in fifteen minutes and the lowest fare was 6d. In the two years ending 1840, many thousands of passengers had travelled on the line.

In 1871 the Midland Westgate station, the original Sheffield and Rotherham Railway terminus, was closed for passengers, to be used instead for 'goods, corn etc'.

REF 14187   *Westgate Railway Station 1910-1920*

Gummer recalled Westgate station as having a large hall providing facilities for booking. The sloping covered gangway, giving access to the platform, was unpopular with passengers and was replaced with a temporary wooden building.

The new station building opened November 1871 in Main Street, a new road off Westgate. Passengers were expected to await the arrival of the trains in the waiting rooms 'appropriate to the classes' after obtaining their tickets. The single fares were now, first class 6d, second class 5d and third class 4d from Westgate to Sheffield.

The new building was said to be 'of no credit to the railway' and Sir Charles Stoddart named it 'The Rabbit Hutch' and declared that it 'offended our senses and should be removed'.

The 'rabbit hutch' was to outlive the railway and finished its life as a market-traders store.

REF 03511   *View of 'The Rabbit Hutch' from Don Street 1900-1901*
Guest and Chrimes Exhibition Horse and Float

As locomotive 40409 left Westgate at 5.27pm on 4th October 1952 this marked the closure of the station 114 years after it opened.

REF 06633

Mayor, Councillor M W Young & Driver of the last train
Inset picture Railway Ticket 4th October 1952

Reproduced by kind permission of Mr R Bye

Waggonettes leaving Edwards Bros' Motor Garage at 9 Horace Street for an outing. Aboard are Arthur Broomhead and Thomas Edwards who lived at 38 & 40 Westgate.

During the summer months it was custom for many firms to give their employees a day out. Messrs Moorhouse of Rotherham provided transport for such trips consisting of omnibuses and waggonettes. During the summer of 1877 they advertised trips each week to Roche Abbey leaving from The Ship Inn Yard Westgate. During October these were discontinued 'for the season'.

TRAMWAYS

REF 00152   *Tram travelling from Westgate, through Westgate Green towards Canklow*

During October 1899 Rotherham Corporation published its initial proposals to apply for Parliamentary permission to build several tramways, one of which was from Westgate along Main Street to Masbrough station.

In November 1899 they asked for powers to build a line which would pass through Templeborough to Westgate and beyond and from Canklow to a junction with the line from Sheffield at Westgate. The two bills received Royal Assent in July 1900.

Little happened until the matter was raised in the town council towards the end of 1901. Among other improvements, road widening was needed in Westgate. The following February a tramway to Tinsley was added to the specification. Some councillors objected to this, feeling that they should discourage the Rotherham residents from going to Sheffield and spending their money there.

The Electric & Light Tramway Committee' was formed to implement the powers obtained. Tramcars were running along Westgate from 1903 and commenced on the Canklow route 6th June 1903 to Canklow via High Street, Westgate & Canklow Road. The route to Templeborough via High Street, Westgate & Sheffield Road commenced 11th June 1903 and the line extended to Tinsley 21st September 1903.

REF 02486   *1907-1915 Double ended tram, Main Street*

The tracks originally laid in Main Street included points which allowed the trams to turn right into Westgate. Early morning services were provided for the use of miners travelling to Rotherham Main Colliery at Canklow from the Masbrough district. This was short lived, as colliers preferred to walk into Westgate to catch the Canklow tram, thus saving a penny.

Single ended tram stopping outside Westgate Station for passengers to alight

The Corporation obtained powers to run Trolley vehicles from 1912. In 1931 the conversion of Trams to Trolley buses began. The installation of Trolley bus wiring from Westgate to Templeborough was undertaken in 1938/9. Trolley buses [or Tracklesses as they were locally known] commenced on this route in March 1940 and continued until 1949. Elsewhere in Rotherham Trolley buses ran until 1965.

The joint tramcar service operating between Rotherham & Sheffield continued until December 1948 and then converted to motor buses.

Tramcars operated between Rotherham & Templeborough for a further year.

The 10.42pm tram from Templeborough to Rotherham on the night of the 13th November 1949 [with an unofficial fare of 1d] brought to an end the Tramcar era.

As one era ended another began - 'The Bus'

The first Crossley buses were used as replacement vehicles for the tramcars, arriving in April 1949. They were allocated to the '69' Rotherham to Sheffield route for the following 15 years.

Reproduced by kind permission of Mr W Ryan   *HET 513, 1965*

The '69' bus is shown travelling up Corporation Street and would have journeyed via Westgate and onto Sheffield. The Odeon and Topps store are shown to the left of the picture and The Turf Tavern [Hammond Ales] to the right.

Although this bus was numerically the penultimate in the Rotherham fleet, it was the last Crossley bus to be built, leaving the factory at Stockport in 1953.

HET 513 was subsequently presented to the British Transport Commission for preservation.

Reproduced by kind permission of Mr H Turner   *HET 514 Route 69, on Sheffield Road approaching Templeborough*

The two Crossley buses following each other along this busy route to the steelworks are approaching Bow Bridge on Sheffield Road. To the left is the Don Forge Chimney and on the skyline above Westgate, the Old Chapel Downs Row is visible.

HET 512,
Route 70, to Templeborough, via Westgate and Sheffield Road.

T. CHARLES

TAKES THIS OPPORTUNITY OF THANKING THE NOBILITY, GENTRY, AN[D]
TRADESPEOPLE FOR THEIR LIBERAL SUPPORT IN THE PAST, AND TRUST[S]
THAT THEY WILL STILL CONTINUE THEIR PATRONAGE.

T. C. HAS A STAFF OF SKILLED WORKMEN IN EVERY BRANCH OF THE TRAD[E]
AND A WELL-SELECTED STOCK OF DRY TIMBER, WHICH ENABLES HIM T[O]
WARRANT EVERY ARTICLE HE MANUFACTURES.

BROUGHAMS, LANDAUS, VICTORIAS, DOG CARTS, & PONY CART[S]
ALL THE LATEST LONDON DESIGNS IN STOCK, OR BUILT
TO ORDER.

WARRANTED FOR 12 MONTHS.

T. CHARLES IS SOLE AGENT IN ROTHERHAM FOR THE UP-TO-DATE
CANADIAN GIGS AND CARS.
ELEGANT, LIGHT, AND DURABLE.   VERY CHEAP.   SEND FOR DESIGN[S]
PRICES, AND FULL PARTICULARS.

T. CHARLES,
CARRIAGE BUILDER,
SHEFFIELD ROAD,
ROTHERHAM.

Slaters directory 1887 advertised Thomas Charles as 'Coach and Carriage Builders'. They obtained a prize medal at the Wentworth & District Exibition. Estimates and designs were free of charge by applying to the Rotherham & West Riding Carriage Works, Sheffield Road.

By 1905 they are listed in Whites Directory as West Riding Carriage & Motor Works continuing until 1916.

Kellys 1922 Directory shows The West Riding Motor Co as authorised Ford dealers Sheffield Road and Westgate.

Both T Charles and The West Riding Motor Co appeared to operate from the same location on Sheffield Road.

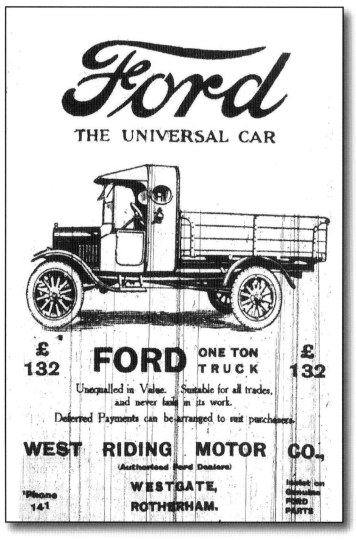

J. CLAYTON AND SONS THE MOTOR HOUSE, WESTGATE

The business run by the Clayton family became known as the 100% Austin Dealers. Around 1922 the cost of an Austin 7 was £230. A decade later the price reduced to £120.

J Clayton & Sons Ltd established the business in 1921 and continued for 60 years until it closed in 1981.

RILEY'S COACHES WESTGATE

Mr Cecil Riley was born in 1896 and began working in the Transport business in 1923 with a covered wagon. He used this to take miners to work at Thurcroft Colliery returning to Rotherham with a load of coal. He bought his first 20 seater coach in 1927 and his business went from strength to strength

Cecil Riley is listed in Kelly's Directories from 1925-1932 at 75 & 77 Westgate and from 1933-1934 at 110 Westgate. In addition, 1935 shows Cecil Riley Haulage Contractor [Garage] between 76 & 84 Westgate continuing until the early 1950's. Eventually in 1948 110 Westgate is listed as Westgate Riley's [Motors] Motor Coach Booking Office.

In 1954 the garage is showing between 78-84 Westgate but the booking office disappeared from 110 and moved into Corporation Street.

The garage continued to be listed in Kelly's until the 1970's.

In 1938 Mr Riley applied to the Yorkshire Traffic Commissioners for permission to vary conditions of a licence, to allow him to operate transport services to the away matches of Rotherham United.

Many people had approached him to run excursions to the football matches, such was the support for Rotherham United. This would also enable the followers to return home immediately after the match.

Two Railway Companies opposed the application, however, demand dictated there should be a road service available.

RFHS

During World War Two the coach firm ran vehicles to the steel works and throughout the region on a Government contract.

Reminiscent of Cup-Tie queues, people began to gather at 10.30pm.one evening in February 1949 outside the booking office of C. Riley, Westgate, for the opportunity to book for his summer excursions to Cleethorpes, Skegness and Mablethorpe.

People brought camping stools, flasks and refreshments. Though booking did not commence until 9am the following day there were over 300 people in the queue by 6am, with more arriving. Many of the tickets available for the middle of summer were sold during the day and 310 bookings were recorded during the first four hours. One woman took it in turns with her husband to queue overnight, while another woman was so cold with the length of the wait that she was unable to open her purse.

Mr Riley died in 1978.

TRANSPORT REFERENCE
FRONTISPIECE PHOTOGRAPHS - ROTHERHAM ARCHIVES & LOCAL STUDY SERVICE
WESTGATE RAILWAY STATION BRIDGE 1858-1867 REF 06637 PHOTOGRAPHER UNKNOWN
SHEFFIELD & ROTHERHAM RAILWAY MUG 1838 REF 10366
PHOTOGRAPHER UNKNOWN

1] EARLY COACHES
   HALL CC ROTHERHAM & DISTRICT TRANSPORT VOL 1 1996
   PARNHAM JACK -WATERLOOS- FROM HIS WESTGATE FILE
   SMITH HOWARD A HISTORY OF ROADS & TRANSPORT 1992 - WATERLOOS
   ROTHERHAM ADVERTISER 4/10/1952 ARTICLE BY DOROTHY GREENE

   ADVERTISEMENTS
   CRITERION, SHEFFIELD & ROTHERHAM- SHEFFIELD IRIS 25/10/1834
   EXPEDITIOUS TRAVELLING- SHEFFIELD IRIS 13/11/1838
   RAILWAY CONVEYANCE & CARRIERS DRAKES DIRECTORY 1862

2] SHEFFIELD & ROTHERHAM RAILWAY
   HALL CC ROTHERHAM & DISTRICT TRANSPORT VOL 1 1996
   RMBC INTERNET INFORMATION S&R RAILWAY
   GUMMER G REMINISCENCES OF ROTHERHAM 1927

   ADVERTISEMENTS
   SHEFFIELD & ROTHERHAM RAILWAY SHEFFIELD IRIS 20/11/1838
   DODDS & SON ENGINEERS & MILLWRIGHTS- DRAKES DIRECTORY 1862

   PHOTOGRAPHS
   ROTHERHAM ARCHIVES & LOCAL STUDY SERVICE
   WESTGATE STATION MAP 1851 REF 06649 PHOTOGRAPHER UNKNOWN
   WESTGATE RAILWAY STATION 1910-1920 REF 14187 PHOTOGRAPHER
   UNKNOWN
   THE RABBIT HUTCH 1900 REF 03511 PHOTOGRAPHER LMA
   LAST TRAIN FROM WESTGATE REF 06633 PHOTOGRAPHER UNKNOWN

   S & R RAILWAY COAT OF ARMS MR D BIRCH

   RAILWAY TICKET   MR R BYE

3] PHOTOGRAPH – WAGGONETTES – M JACKSON

4] TRAMS
   HALL CC ROTHERHAM & DISTRICT TRANSPORT VOL 1 1996
   PAUL FOX INFORMATION
   ROTHERHAM ADVERTISER 14/9/1901
   RMBC DIAMOND JUBILEE BOOKLET 1903-1963 ROTHERHAM ARCHIVES
   RMBC 50 YEARS OF PASSENGER TRANSPORT ROTHERHAM ARCHIVES

   PHOTOGRAPHS—
   ROTHERHAM ARCHIVES & LOCAL STUDY SERVICE
   TRAM TRAVELLING THROUGH WESTGATE GREEN REF 00152
   PHOTOGRAPHER
   GW KNAPTON [LMA]
   TRAM MAIN STREET REF 02486 EL SCRIVENS 172-105 [LMA]

   SINGLE ENDED TRAM- S L SMITH FROM THE COLLECTION OF PAUL FOX

5] BUSES
   PAUL FOX INFORMATION
   LUMB GEOFF 'THE HEYDAY OF THE BUS 1996
   [BRITISH TRANSPORT COMMISSION]

   PHOTOGRAPHS – MR W RYAN HET 513 MR H TURNER HET 512 & 514

6] ADVERTISEMENTS
   T CHARLES ROTHERHAM WEEKLY NEWS 15/04/1899
   WEST RIDING CO ROTHERHAM ADVERTISER 25/04/1925
   INFORMATION-DIRECTORIES - ARCHIVES & LOCAL STUDIES ROTHERHAM
   J CLAYTON & SONS RHAM ADVERTISER 13/04/1935,11/12/1981

7] COACHES
   C RILEY COACH OPERATOR- ROTHERHAM ADVERTISER
   12/11/1938,/26/02/1949, 14/07/1978
   PHOTOGRAPH
   ROTHERHAM FAMILY HISTORY SOCIETY
   C RILEY WESTGATE GARAGE [PART PHOTOGRAPH]

Six

Trade and Commerce

The Rotherham Co-operative Society February 1927

THE CO-OPERATIVE SOCIETY - WESTGATE 1909

The Co-operative buildings originally belonged to Mr Appleyard of Conisbro' and were built for his extensive furnishing business, afterwards known as Johnson and Appleyard. The premises of Myers and Kay on the site of the old Post office at 5 Westgate were also acquired by the Co-operative Society in 1900. During the construction of Corporation Street in 1904, 1& 3 Westgate were subsequently rebuilt and that too became part of the Co-op.

Masbro' Equitable Pioneer Society founded in 1869 became Rotherham Co-operative Society when they moved into the Main Street premise in 1925.

In 1909 Masbro' Equitable Society celebrated the opening of large extensions on the corner of Westgate and Domine Lane.

Situated in the basement, the restaurant comprised a dining room, tearoom, smoke room, grill room and kitchen. The principal rooms were furnished with panelled oak dado, the ceilings with enriched mouldings and the floor was 'Terrazzo pavement in patterns'. Patrons approached the restaurant from an entrance on Domine Lane.

The ground floor divided into three shops, the corner for furnishing and the other two for butchery and fish & game. The frontage of the furniture shop to both streets was used for show purposes with large plate glass windows and an entrance lobby. The first floor contained the furnishing department whilst the second floor was used as a furniture storeroom.

The upper exterior of the building complimented the adjoining premises with Stoke Hall stone, pilasters, cornices etc and finished with open moulded parapets and pediment at the corner. The stall boards and pilasters to the shops were Labrador polished granite and the roofs covered with Westmorland slate.

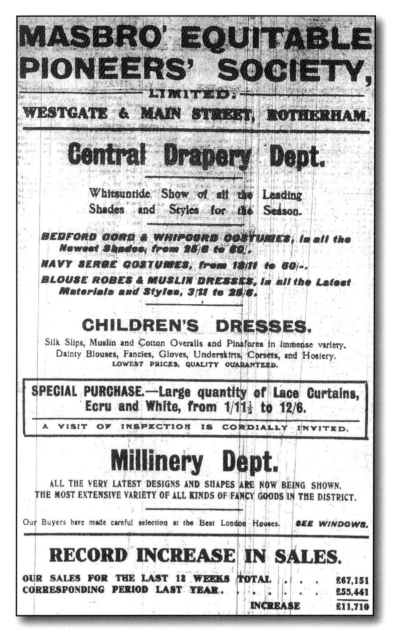

1913

The property would enable almost every business that was required for a household to be carried on, and that site was acknowledged to be the best in Rotherham.

John Platt the 18th century architect built himself a house in Westgate, the remains of which are on the site of the Co-operative Society buildings.

'THE NEW CAFÉ'

By 1927 major alterations were taking place within the premises to change an unused area 'from a place of dust and gloom into a bright and spacious restaurant and café.'

Previously situated in the basement, the restaurant, café and kitchens were transferred to the top floor of the building. Originally approached via Domine Lane, a new entrance was made direct from Westgate.

Improvements were also made to the provisions and grocery departments on the ground floor, these were combined and installed with new fittings.

Customers approached the restaurant through a tiled lobby into an entrance hall, containing a wide oak staircase and electric lift. On the first floor, to the right and left of the new staircase were the furnishing showrooms with the new restaurant situated on the second floor. This comprised of two large dining rooms [average size 45ft by 25ft each] one of which could be separately used for private social functions.

The restaurant was panelled in light oak, the ceilings were of dark timbers with plaster between them and the windows had steel casements and leaded lights. The staircase window displayed the arms of both town and the society. There was a lounge for writing and smoking, cloakroom, and a new exit staircase. The electric fittings were in antique bronze metal and the decorations, 'bright and cheerful.'

A special service room provided with double servery doors [which opened into each restaurant] contained a 'washing apparatus' for cleaning crockery. The kitchen, behind this room was fully tiled from floor to ceiling in white glazed tiles, well lit and ventilated, and contained the most up-to-date cookers, ovens and hot closets. 'All cooking to be done by gas'.

ROTHERHAM CO-OPERATIVE SOCIETY LTD.

ESTABLISHED	1869
MEMBERSHIP	28,500
ANNUAL BUSINESS	£800,000
MEMBERS' SHARE CAPITAL	£730,000
MEMBERS' LOAN CAPITAL	£145,000
SOCIETY'S INVESTMENTS	£870,000
SOCIETY'S RESERVE FUND	£65,000

Our Reputation has been built up on the supply of goods Produced Under Ideal Conditions and Trade Union Principles, at Reasonable Prices and the Best of Service.

THE RECORD AMOUNT OF £46,000 WAS PAID OUT TO MEMBERS OF THE 3½d. CLUB IN NOVEMBER.

GUARD THE HEALTH OF YOUR FAMILY —DRINK PASTEURISED MILK.

A DIVIDEND OF 2/- IN THE £

HAS BEEN PAID ON MEMBERS' PURCHASES FOR THE LAST EIGHTEEN HALF-YEARS.

The Benefits paid to Members last year by way of Dividend, Interests, and Collective Life Assurance totalled £115,080.

Join the Society and Share in the Wonderful Benefits only enjoyed by Co-operators.

1937

59

WESTGATE POST OFFICE

In 1859 Rotherham Post Office transferred from High Street to new premises at 5 Westgate.

A hundred years earlier, evidence of a Post Office facility or 'Receiving House' in Rotherham is a letter dated 18th August 1735 bearing a Rotherham hand stamp.

In 1750 William Wilson licensee of the Angel Hotel in High Street is recorded as Postmaster, Publican, Bookseller and Stationer. The Angel is described as 'a large Postal establishment where many coaches stopped for a fresh supply of horses and for passengers to refresh themselves' before continuing their journey.

In 1762 son William became Postmaster at the Angel Hotel and in 1780 upon his death, his wife Sarah became Postmistress. She in turn was succeeded by her two daughters Catherine and Martha in 1786.

In 1796 Martha became sole Postmistress and during that year proposals were made that 'Rotherham sub office to Sheffield' be made a 'Post Town'. Full Post Office status took place between March and July. Miss Wilson was reported as being 'sufficiently instructed' and was appointed 11th March 1796. It was thought that she probably moved the Post Office to premises next door to The Three Cranes in High Street at that time.

Due to increased business Martha Wilson was assisted by clerk Robert Morton. During one week in 1838 a total of 927 letters were posted in Rotherham and in 1845 Sunday evening deliveries of letters in Rotherham were discontinued at the request of the townsfolk.

Martha retained this appointment until her death in 1847 aged 85 years. She was seen as a kindly person and enlisted the help of wealthy local residents to pay postage for the poorer townsfolk, 'for occasional needful letters to distant relatives'.

Mary Ann Jackson the great niece of Martha Wilson continued the tradition of Postmistress until her marriage in 1853 to Joseph Owen who then became Postmaster.

In 1859 Rotherham Post Office transferred from High Street to new premises at 5 Westgate. Post Office Savings Bank business commenced on 23rd October 1861 and the influence of the railways on the transport of mail increased the postal work during 1862. It was at this time that posting boxes were introduced, the colour 'pillar box red' being adopted in 1874. Walled pillar-boxes were installed in Westgate in 1862. In 1870 the Post Office Telegraph opened.

Joseph Owen remained in charge until his death in 1873 when his wife became Postmistress again.

In 1880 the Post Office moved to the Midland Railway buildings which were erected in 1838 as part of the Westgate terminus of the Sheffield and Rotherham Railway. The GPO's proposal to utilise these premises caused much dissention in the town. Meetings were held and High Street and College Street were named as more central. In spite of protests the GPO took the premises on a lease and altered them for their purpose.`

REF 00120   *Postmen outside the Westgate Post Office 1887-1897*

By the time Mrs Owen retired in 1887 after a service of 52 years, [an appointment having been in the family for nearly 150 years] there were 40 staff in the Westgate head office and 34 sub-offices. The head office dealt with five-and-a-half million letters per year.

The Post Office moved again in March 1907 to purpose built premises in Main Street. Past and present postal employees gathered in the old post office room in Westgate and formed a procession to the new building.

About 3,000 people assembled in the vicinity to watch the Mayor, Colonel C J Stoddart insert a silver gilt key in the door of the new building. Alderman Gummer dispatched the first paid telegram from the new premises.

POST OFFICE,

5, WESTGATE.—MR. JOSEPH R. OWEN, POSTMASTER.

LETTERS ARE DISPATCHED

To Rugby, all parts of the South-Eastern Counties, Birmingham, Belper, Derby, Chesterfield, and Sheffield at 1.30 A.M. and 10.55 P.M.

To Barnsley, Leeds, Huddersfield, Halifax, Bradford, Wakefield, Hull, Gainsbro', Worksop, Sheffield, and Scotland at 1.30 a.m.

To Bawtry, Tickhill, Maltby, and Wickersley at 5 a.m.

To Doncaster, Thorne, Hatfield, Conisbro', Hooton Roberts, and Country at 5 a.m.

London Morning Mail, 9.45 a.m.

To Scarbro', York, Durham, Northumberland, and part of Scotland at 11.40 a.m.

To Barnsley, Doncaster, Leeds, Wakefield, Huddersfield, Halifax, and Sheffield at 2.15 p.m.

To Ireland and Lancashire at 7 p.m.

To Manchester, Liverpool, and the Isle of Man at 8.50 p.m.

To Alfreton, Belper, Birmingham, Sheffield, Bakewell, Chesterfield, Derby, London, and the Eastern, Western, Midland, and Southern Counties, Guernsey and Jersey at 10.55 p.m.

DELIVERY.—There are two deliveries by letter carriers at 7.30 a.m. and 3.15 p.m.

Messengers are dispatched daily to Parkgate, Rawmarsh, Swinton, Wath, Greasbro' Wentworth, Elsecar, Kimberworth, Thorpe Hesley, Canklow, Brinsworth, Catcliffe, Treeton, Woodhouse Mill, Whiston, Ulley, Aston, Wales, Tinsley, Brightside, and Shiregreen.

The Office opens at 7.30 a.m. and closes at 10 p.m. On Sundays it is opened at 8 a.m. and closes at 10 a.m.

There are two Branch Offices, one at 34, College-road, Masbro', and the other at Parkgate. There is also a receiving box at Masbro' Station; and pillar letter boxes are stationed at the Rawmarsh-lane end, and in Alma-road, Moorgate.

JOSEPH FRANCE (LTD)

The business established in 1872 by Joseph France in Millgate transferred to the Baths Works, Westgate before their extensive paint & and varnish works were built in Oil Mill Fold. A limited company was formed in July 1932 which manufactured all classes of decorators industrial parts and varnishes for railway wagons.

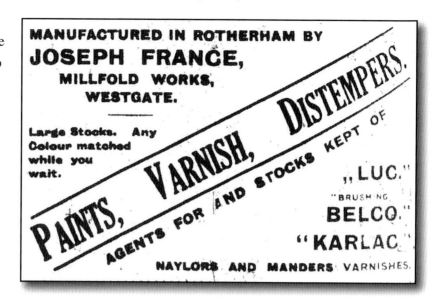

They also had a large business in motor dynamo, lubricating oils and greases.

The business was divided into two sections, paint and varnish manufacture and oil blending. The oil department was on a site previously used as an Oil Mill many years before.

The warehouses of Joseph France were adjacent to the Baths Inn beerhouse and the Baths Foundry. During April 1877 clouds of smoke were seen entering the lower apartments of the beerhouse. Investigation showed that oil and paraffin stored in the warehouse were alight and a serious fire had broken out.

A large crowd of spectators gathered in Westgate to watch, as The Sun Fire Brigade and the Borough Fire Brigade fought the blaze. Hoses belonging to both Brigades and lengths of hose borrowed from the Workhouse were used. The fire had engulfed the stock and efforts were concentrated on saving the surrounding buildings. It was thought impossible to save the beerhouse at one stage, and occupants threw their furniture and belongings out of the upstairs windows. This resulted in many articles being badly damaged.

The Baths Foundry was also in danger but eventually the fire was brought under control the following day. The damage was estimated at £2000.

Another prominent decorating business in the 1950s was R J Stokes.

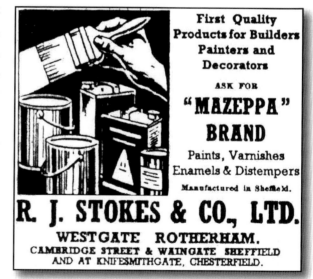

ROBINSON'S FLOUR MILL - WESTGATE

REF 13254

The Rotherham Town Mill, originally a vat-house was converted into a corn mill in 1820 by Messrs J Broadhurst, Son and others. From 1823-1836 it was in the possession of Mr Charles Wright and then taken over by Mr James Hodgson who milled there until his death. The Mill passed to his wife Sarah until the coming of age of her son Mr James Hodgson Jnr. who also worked there until his death in 1874. The business continued a further three years by his Executors when it was taken over by Messrs JW & HR Robinson.

The two brothers bought the premises in 1877 and continually updated the system, putting in new machinery in 1878. Four years later in 1882 the method of milling changed and in 1884 further modernisation was called for.

After visiting Brussells to inspect their methods, the whole of the old stone plant was removed, the mill buildings were raised and new machinery for making flour by the roller process was put down. The system was known as the "gradual reduction system of flour milling"

In 1890 further improvements were made and in 1891 flour milling made advances as the nearly new machinery was re-modelled.

By 1903 another alteration to the machinery was considered necessary. The Rotherham Town Mill could boast that no Flour Mill of its day had more efficient machinery.

The Architect Mr John Platt of Rotherham and Messrs Arnold of Doncaster were commissioned to erect a new silo house for the storage of grain, which would hold 4000 quarters of wheat. Boats laden with grain landed alongside the new silo, the wheat, then raised by means of automatic elevators was distributed to the various silo bins mechanically. The first boatload of wheat delivered by these means was on the 14th June 1896.

In addition to the roller plant Messrs Robinson had a stone plant used for grinding Indian corn and other grains in their fodder department. They also had an electrically heated oven in which to bake samples of bread.

From the time the grain arrived from the River Rother to Robinsons Mills to the time it left as flour it remained untouched by human hand.

In 1901 the firm converted to a Limited Company under Robinson Brothers [Rotherham] Ltd. Mr J. W. Robinson as Chairman and Mr H. R. Robinson as Managing Director.

Due to the ill health of J. W. Robinson in 1907 his brother took sole charge of the business, which he ran assisted by his son Arthur and two nephews R. J. & R. U. Robinson.

Mr Arthur Robinson eventually became Chairman & Managing Director of the firm and in 1936 was elected President of the National Association of British & Irish Millers. He had worked his way up through the mill and office as an ordinary employee.

One feature of the mill was the extent to which laboratory control was carried out. Nothing was left to chance and scientific control was introduced wherever it could be proved of value.

In 1945 the ordinary shares of Robinson Brothers [Rotherham] Ltd were acquired by Hovis Ltd.

THE OLD BREWERY

HAS SERVED ROTHERHAM FOR MORE THAN 110 YEARS

Modern Hygienic Plant and Long Brewing Experience ensure
Wholesome and Invigorating Beverages of Guaranteed Purity

NATIVE OR VISITOR IS AGREED THAT

BETTER BEER IS NOT BREWED

(ON DRAUGHT OR IN BOTTLE)

BENTLEY'S, ROTHERHAM

BENTLEY'S BREWERY

Robert Bentley was born in 1799, the son of Timothy Bentley, founder of the Brewery. He moved to Rotherham in the 1820's to run the business and when Timothy died in 1830 Robert inherited the brewery.

He built three large detached houses adjacent to the brewery for himself and members of his family, West House, Mill House and Westville and lived in West House following his marriage. Robert improved Westgate Farm situated on the opposite side of the road and built a Maltings higher up Westgate.

RFHS COLIN LEONARD   *The Maltings*

William Oakley recorded in his journal that in 1830 a cannon was fired at 10 o'clock each evening from Bentleys Brewery.

During the Cholera outbreak in 1832/1833 a piece of ground at Park Road, East Dene was given by Robert Bentley for the victims to be buried. The burial ground was sited in fields well away from the edge of town and surrounded by a high brick wall. With the onset of winter the epidemic ended in Rotherham, many of the victims coming from Westgate. The site was again used in a further outbreak in 1849 with many victims coming from the Masbrough area.

[By 1936 houses on the new East Dene Estate were being built close to the burial ground].

Gummer recorded that Bentley's Brewery had its own small fire engine for any emergency at the brewery and assisted the surrounding area when necessary.

Robert who died 28th May 1850 founded the Charity known as 'Bentley's Dole'. He left £3000 vested in the Feoffees of The Common Lands of Rotherham to be distributed according to his will: the interest on £2500 to be divided equally between six poor men and four poor women, the interest on £400 to the Rotherham Dispensary and the interest on £100 to the Wesleyan Benevolent Society.

A memorial to Robert Bentley and his family is adjacent to the South Transept in the Minster Church, Rotherham.

RFHS COLIN LEONARD

Robert John, son of Robert was born 1822 and took over management of the brewery in the 1840's. Robert John lived at Eastwood House and Finningley Park, Doncaster before returning some years later to live at West House, Westgate. He built a house called The Mount on land at Westgate Farm for his brother-in-law Arthur Hirst who helped him to run the brewery.

Robert John, a prominent person in Rotherham made many donations to the Parish Church and other causes. He was elected Greave of the Rotherham Feoffees in 1853 and 1867. By 1875 Robert John was suffering mental health problems and took no further part in the running of the brewery during the remainder of his life. He died in 1890.

The brewery continued under a board of trustees and was registered as Bentley's Old Brewery [Rotherham] Ltd. in 1949 and taken over by Hammond United Breweries of Bradford in 1956. The Brewery was demolished in 1965.

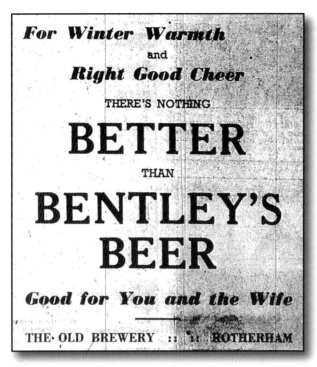

For Winter Warmth
and
Right Good Cheer
THERE'S NOTHING
BETTER
THAN
BENTLEY'S BEER
Good for You and the Wife
THE OLD BREWERY :: :: ROTHERHAM

Ebenezer Elliott wrote a poem referring to Jacob Brettell the Minister of The Old Chapel and to Bentley the Brewer and other well-known people in Rotherham & Sheffield at that time.

'Here's health to our friends of Reform'
then to Palfreyman, Parker and Ward
and Bailey, a star at midday
and Badger, the lawyer, and Brettell the Bard
and Phillips, in battle grown grey;
and Bramhall by bigot un-hung
and Holland, the fearless and pure
and Bramley and Barker- the wise and the young
and Bentley the Rotherham Brewer.

This was published in 'Ivanhoe Review' Volume 1, number 1 January 1898

Price 1d. [page2].

REFERENCE
ROTHERHAM CO-OPERATIVE
GUMMER G REMINISCENCES OF ROTHERHAM 1927
ROTHERHAM ADVERTISER 10/04/1909 PGE 6
NEW CAFÉ-EXTRACT FROM ROTHERHAM ADVERTISER 12/02/1927

ADVERTISEMENTS
ROTHERHAM ADVERTISER-12/02/1927, 10/04/1909, 26/04/1913,
CORONATION SOUVENIR 1937

WESTGATE POST OFFICE
HILL NORMAN POSTAL HISTORY OF ROTHERHAM 1960
GUEST JOHN HISTORIC NOTICES OF ROTHERHAM 1879 PAGE 578
GUMMER G REMINISCENCES OF ROTHERHAM 1927 PAGE 286/287
ROTHERHAM ADVERTISERS- 13/06/1874, 27/06/1874, 31/07/1886, 31/05/1890, 2/11/1901

PHOTOGRAPH
ROTHERHAM ARCHIVES & LOCAL STUDY SERVICE
WESTGATE POST OFFICE 1887-1897 REF 00120
PHOTOGRAPHER UNKNOWN

ADVERTISEMENT
DRAKES DIRECTORY 1862
POST OFFICE 5 WESTGATE

JOSEPH FRANCE LTD
ROTHERHAM ADVERTISER 7/04/1877
ROTHERHAM ANNUAL 1939

ADVERTISEMENT
ROTHERHAM ADVERTISER 5/06/1927, 13/3/1954

ROBINSON'S FLOUR MILL
ROTHERHAM ADVERTISER 19/06/1909/PAGE 6, 20/10/1945/PAGE 3,

PHOTOGRAPH
ROTHERHAM ARCHIVES & LOCAL STUDY SERVICES
ROBINSON BROS FLOUR MILL 1934-1936
PHOTOGRAPHER UNKNOWN
REF 13254

ADVERTISEMENT
ROTHERHAM ADVERTISER CORONATION SOUVENIR 1937

BENTLEYS BREWERY
ROTHERHAM ADVERTISER 26/01/1867 pge 4, 6/09/1890 pge5, 23/11/1867 pge1
ROTHERHAM ARCHIVES- ARCHIVE LIST 2 86/B, LIST 3 186/F
WHITES DIRECTORY 1902
OAKLEY WILLIAM YE OLDE ROTHERHAM TOWN 1915
THE FEOFFEES OF THE COMMON LANDS OF ROTHERHAM

ILLUSTRATION
SUPPLIED BY JIM CLARKE

PHOTOGRAPHS
ROTHERHAM FAMILY HISTORY SOCIETY
THE MALTHOUSE PHOTOGRAPHER COLIN LEONARD
BENTLEYS BREWERY PHOTOGRAPHER COLIN LEONARD

ADVERTISEMENT
ROTHERHAM ADVERTISER 12/11/1938

Seven

Public Houses

REF 00137

SHIP HOTEL WESTGATE 1840

WESTGATE PUBLIC HOUSES

Westgate was supplied with many public houses and beer houses during the 19th century. Some have changed their names over the years whilst others have disappeared, however one or two still remain.

ALMA TAVERN
25 Westgate
Earliest date 1860
Rebuilt 1908

Licensees
George Neatby 1860-1869
Hannah Neatby 1870-1899

In 1720 this site was the dwelling house of the Minister of The Old Chapel Downs Row. The land comprising 925 sq yds was leased to George Neatby in 1854.

REF 15670

BARREL, Westgate Green

Earliest date 1819 sold to Thomas Green Innkeeper in 1819

BATH INN, 43 Westgate

Opened 1852 closed 1935 Named after the public baths in Westgate which also gave its name to the Baths foundry

Licensees
1852-63 Henry Smith
1864-73 Henry T Smith
1877-80 James Curtis

Licensees Henry T Smith 1864-1873 also ran a brewing business next door to the Bath Inn and James Curtis 1877-1880 ran a lodging house at 56 Westgate opposite the Inn.

CUTLERS ARMS,
29 Westgate

Earliest date 1825
Rebuilt 1866 and 1907

Licensees
1825-37   Benjamin Flockton
1852-62   Henry Wood
1887-1912 Patrick Fenoughty

RFHS

The current building dates from 1907 and has an interior lobby with mosaic tile floor and green tiled walls leading to an inner door with brass fittings and stained glass overlight. All the stained glass is green foliage and yellow flowers in the Art Nouveau style. The rebuilding of the Cutlers Arms in 1907 facilitated a widening of Westgate to relieve traffic congestion.

The Cutlers Arms is a listed building.

DUKE OF YORK
Westgate

1825

This Inn stood on the site of Westgate station and was demolished to make way for the Sheffield and Rotherham Railway terminus opened in 1838.

DUSTY MILLER
77/Westgate/1Canklow Road

Earliest date 1822

Original building faced
Sheffield Road
Present building erected 1894

Licensees

1822-1823 John Mellor
1849-1862 James Dobb
1863-1875 Edward Lenton

Dusty Miller Circa 1891-1895

REF 00132

LITTLE SWANN, 58 Westgate

opened 1851 - closed 1868

A small beer house previously known as the Welsh Lass and the General Moore

Licensees

1851 William Stone, 1861-1864 Joseph Hutton, 1865- 1868 Richard Hague

PRINCE OF WALES FEATHERS
84 Westgate

Earliest date 1856

Licensees

1856-1860 James Holland

1861-1868 John Steer

1869-1879 Henry J Wright

RFHS COLIN LEONARD

ROYAL OAK

Earliest Date 1766 - closed prior to 1777

The Station Inn at 16 Westgate 1868-1885 formally known as The Royal Oak.

SHIP HOTEL, 2 Westgate

Earliest date 1682 Closed 1933. Sold by Feoffees of the Common lands to Rotherham Corporation for street improvement.

Licensees

1682   John Gibson

1849-1852 Robert Spendlove

1862-1868 Matthew G Mallinson

Ship Hotel 1880-1882
REF 14227

STATION HOTEL, 16 Westgate

Earliest date 1839/1840

Built opposite the Westgate terminus of the Sheffield and Rotherham Railway. Present building dates from1934/1935 located in a slightly different position nearer to Ship Hill

Licensees

1840-1851 Thomas H Jackson, 1855-1862 Francis Colley, 1895-1911 Joseph Firth

REF 06317   *Station Hotel Circa 1906*

THREE HORSE SHOES

49 Westgate

Earliest Date 1856 - closed March 1931

Licensees

1858-1862 William Hanby

1900-1905 Maria Smith

1925-1931 William H Exley

TRAVELLERS INN
2 Sheffield Road Westgate

Earliest date 1790 Closed 1909
Demolished in the 1920's to improve Westgate/Sheffield Road junction

Licensees

1822-1824 Thomas Badger, 1858-1864 Charles Payne, 1869-1881 George Rylands

REF 00161   *Travellers Inn Circa 1860-1866*

TRUE BRITON INN
78 Westgate

Earliest date 1822
Closed 1923

Licensees
1822-1844 Thomas Smith
1851-1868 Richard Martin
1887-1891 John T Brown

Drawing of True Briton by
Mr J Clarke from a photograph in the
Rotherham Advertiser 22/08/1931

WELLINGTON INN
52 Westgate

Earliest date 1822

The original Wellington Inn dated from 1822 and the present building 1903.

Licencees

1822-1824 Joseph Wild
1861-1868 Robert Poulter
1888-1905 Emma Brown

REF15668

Wellington Inn Circa 1927-1932

WHITE SWAN

71 Westgate

Earliest date 1822

Licensees
1822-1839 Thomas Smith
1861-1863 H Jackson

In 1822 The White Swan was owned by Thomas Smith who also owned the True Briton and other properties on Westgate. Robert Bentley purchased the White Swan in 1848 from William Aizlewood.

The White Swan was the headquarters of the Rotherham Harriers 1895 - 1897 & 1909-1910.

RFHS

REFERENCE

SATTERTHWAITE PAUL ROTHERHAM PUBLIC HOUSES 1820-1990 [1991]
MR JIM CLARKE

ROTHERHAM ARCHIVES & LOCAL STUDY SERVICE
ROTHERHAM DIRECTORIES

ALMA TAVERN – 2ND SCHEDULE HOLLIS TRUST DEEDS

CUTLERS ARMS
LISTED BUILDINGS REFERENCE BOOK

PHOTOGRAPHS
ROTHERHAM LOCAL ARCHIVES & STUDY SERVICE

ALMA TAVERN	1910-1915	REF 15670
DUSTY MILLER	1891-1895	REF 00132
SHIP HOTEL	1840	REF 00137
SHIP HOTEL	1880-1882	REF 14227
WELLINGTON INN	1927-1932	REF 15668
STATION HOTEL	1907	REF 06317
TRAVELLERS INN	1860-1866	REF 00161

 The above photographs are by unknown photographers

ROTHERHAM FAMILY HISTORY SOCIETY
PRINCE OF WALES FEATHERS PHOTOGRAPHER COLIN LEONARD
CUTLERS ARMS
WHITE SWAN

DRAWING OF TRUE BRITON BY MR J CLARKE
FROM A PHOTOGRAPH IN ROTHERHAM ADVERTISER 22/08/1931

Eight

Conditions

REF 15723   *Barker's Row Westgate 1910-1912*

WESTGATE SLUM CONDITIONS

During the nineteenth century some of the worst slum conditions in Rotherham were to be found in the town centre.

Westgate was made up of a number of courtyards on either side of the road. These were hidden behind the facades of shop frontages and town houses. Developers had crammed as many cottages as possible onto available land. They were ill lit and without proper sanitation and all suffered from poor ventilation.

In 1832 Rotherham suffered a cholera outbreak with many of the victims coming from Westgate.

The Town Council met during August 1898 to discuss the proposed demolition of insanitary dwellings in Westgate, and the erection of a 'Model Lodging House'. The Public Health Committee recommended the purchase of ten cottages and 1950 yards of land for the sum of £600.

A large number of people were constantly passing through the town and taking up temporary residence. It was estimated that approximately 400 people were living in lodging houses. A case of smallpox had come from Middlesbro' into a lodging house in Rotherham. Fortunately the person recovered but this was used as an example to show that conditions must be improved.

The courts, some named after the men who built them, Styring's yard and Wild's yard. True Briton's Yard named after the public house and All Nations Yard probably named after the different individuals that lived there.

From time to time the yards changed their names, Styrings yard became Court Six and Wild's yard became Court eight. Courts six, seven and eight were where the Telephone Exchange is now sited.

One of the main problems in the town was lack of proper drainage for sewage. A public drain had been constructed in Oil Mill Fold but in most cases the existing drains were above the floor level of the cellars and subject to flooding.

By the early 1930's slum clearance had commenced and the courts along Westgate were being swept away. In 1933 the Medical Officer of Health described the conditions he found in a house of two occupants in Court 8:

The house had two rooms, one up and one down and opened onto a court shared by 12 houses. Entrance to the court was by way of a 3ft wide passage. The house had no rear door or rear windows and a northerly aspect. The rooms were low with no through ventilation. They were damp and in a bad state of repair. There were no facilities for washing clothes and no food storage.

Court 8 (Wild's Yard)
prior to demolition 1933

REF 00147

The closet accommodation was insufficient and insanitary. Four houses in the court were infested with bugs.

Notice was also given in 1933 for the clearance of Court 6 comprising six dwelling houses, yards, outbuildings and trough closets. There were 31 occupants and the order was given by reason of disrepair or sanitary defects and unfit for human habitation, 644 sq yards in total.

A letter had been written by one of the occupants of Court six, Three Horse Shoe Yard to the Minister of Health [although it was delivered to the local Sanitary Inspector] seeking help to repair his oven and fireplace because he was having to buy shop bread to feed his family of six instead of baking their own. The tenant explained that they also couldn't bake meat pies because of the smoke causing them all to suffer with sore eyes. He concluded by saying he didn't know how they kept their health.

An example of the houses in Court Six numbered from 5-10:

House 5
Rent 6/8d weekly
Husband, wife and child under 10 years - Kitchen + 2 Bedrooms and Scullery
Conclusion when inspected - Very dirty, Bugs and Fleas

House 6
Rent 7/- weekly
Two Adults
Cleanliness Fair - Bugs, Fleas, Cockroaches and Rats

House 7
Rent 5/7d weekly
Occupants - 2 males 3 females - [2 children 1 lodger] - Kitchen + 1 bedroom
Cleanliness Satisfactory - Bugs Fleas Cockroaches, Rats

House 8
Rent 6/- weekly
Kitchen, Scullery, 2 Bedrooms
Cleanliness Fair - Bugs, Fleas and Rats

House 9
Rent 7/- weekly
Kitchen, Scullery, 2 Bedrooms
Cleanliness Fair - Bugs, Fleas and Rats

House 10
Rent 6/- weekly
Occupant—one
Kitchen, 1 Bedroom
Cleanliness Fair - Bugs

Number 47 Westgate was refused registration as a Common Lodging house and the property vacated in 1932. The police were asked to assist and ensure the premises were not occupied. Number 49 Westgate formally known as The Three Horseshoes was also vacated and included in the Westgate Court 6 Clearance.

Mappins Brewery who owned 78 Westgate, known as 'The Old True Briton' objected to the Clearance order 1937. The Corporation required the site for their road widening scheme.

Formally a public house now used as a dwelling house and let as a Common Lodging house it had 12 rooms with 10 families and 45 occupants. This was not classed as overcrowding but because it was internally badly designed thought a case for inclusion.

Objections were made in as far as the house part of the premises were concerned. The adjoining building was completely self-contained and hired out as a club or recreation room. This room was previously used as a place of worship.

After a local enquiry in 1937 the owners agreed to demolish the front part and use the large room at the rear for meetings but not habitation.

Courts 13 & 14 came under the Clearance Order 1937 and were demolished in 1938.

ROTHERHAM'S LABOUR EXCHANGE

The new Labour Exchange in Rotherham was established in the old Post Office in Westgate. The frontage of the building had been altered sometime earlier in the Westgate widening scheme and extensive additions and alterations made for its new purpose, with separate entrances for men, and women including boys under seventeen years of age.

REF 00119   *Labour Exchange Westgate 1910-1920*

The Mayor, Mr D Mullins and Mr W Milnes the Manager walked in procession and opened the Labour Exchange on 1st February 1910.

The Labour Exchange Act had come into force whereby " Employers in want of workers could find just the workers they needed, and the unemployed men could be placed in communication with employers wherever there was a demand for workers. The benefits would be infinite and save the hopeless degrading tramp from workshop to workshop in search of employment".

In 1931 there were 10,436 on the unemployment register. By 1938 a new Labour Exchange was opened in Moorgate. It was said, "At the old building, everyone passing could see the unemployed entering, the new building would not expose the men to public gaze".

The ground floor of the Labour Exchange subsequently became the British Rail local area control room responsible for the day to day running of the railway for Rotherham, Sheffield, Chesterfield and Barnsley on the old Midland line. Engine men, guards relief and arranging special trains such as freight trains to Nottingham were controlled from there.

The control office continued until the 1960's when it transferred to Sheffield.

HOUSE OF HELP FOR GIRLS

The founder of The House of Help for Girls was Miss Florence Falding, daughter of Dr Falding, Principal of Rotherham Congregational College. She recognised that something needed to be done to improve the lives of poorer working girls.

In 1884 a Girls Club was formed and met each evening from 7–9pm in a room at the house of Mrs Addy, Westfield View, Westgate. The girls enjoyed games and singing and were taught sewing. The club did not meet there for very long and moved to a two-roomed rented house in Burrells Row, Westgate. Here, there was no caretaker to help keep the girls in order and they took delight in frightening and shocking the ladies in charge. Eventually most girls settled happily and recognised their opportunity to get situations and better themselves, which was difficult without suitable clothes and training. It was common practice for the ladies in charge to visit Pawn Shops and retrieve the girl's best coat or dress just before sending her to a situation. No permanent good could be done for the girls unless a home was found where they could be trained and supplied with clothes.

REF 15862   *Smiths Pawn Brokers, Westgate 1903-1907*

The next move was to 44 Westgate where a 'good house' was rented and Mrs Addy installed as caretaker. The club, held in a large room at the top of the yard soon moved into the house, which possessed a piano. The girls loved singing hymns and cheerful songs.

In 1890 the House of Help suffered a crisis. Funds were low and expenses great, causing a detrimental effect on the work there. The Rev W.Law, Vicar of Rotherham and Chairman of the society had great sympathy with this work and was determined it should not be given up without a struggle. One of the committee members, Mrs Nightingale, suggested holding a sale of work and Mr Styring's Auction Room in Moorgate Street was loaned for the occasion. The first Bazaar, held in December 1890 raised the sum of £90.

A suitable Matron was still needed for the girls but it seemed impossible to offer an adequate salary. The real beginning of the House of Help came when Rev Law persuaded a Miss Washington to offer her services and go and live in the midst of the girls in Westgate.

The Bazaar became an annual fund raising event and subscriptions were started. Annual meetings were held and had visits from many speakers. Opinion changed and connection with the House of Help moved from being unpopular to an honoured position.

In 1892/93 Miss Washington left town and Miss Manico was installed at a salary of £20-£24. The Parish magazine of the time 'Homewords for Hearth & Home' reported that the House of Help was in one of the worst parts of town and linen, furniture, and pictures were needed to brighten up the home.

It had long been felt that the House of Help should be more out of town and away from the girl's surroundings and homes.

The House of Help transferred from 44 Westgate to 36 Nelson Street circa 1898-1901 where the work continued.

REFERENCE
SLUM CONDITIONS
MUNFORD ANTHONY FROM SLUMS TO COUNCIL HOUSES CHAPTER 15 PAGE 273
ASPECTS OF ROTHERHAM 1995
ROTHERHAM ADVERTISER 6/08/1898
ROTHERHAM ARCHIVES & LOCAL STUDY SERVICE
WESTGATE CLEARANCE FILES 1933/1934

PHOTOGRAPHS
ROTHERHAM ARCHIVES & LOCAL STUDY SERVICE
BARKERS ROW 1910-1912 REF 15723 PHOTOGRAPHER UNKNOWN
COURT 8 [WILD'S YARD] 1933 REF 00147 PHOTOGRAPHER UNKNOWN

LABOUR EXCHANGE-
ROTHERHAM ADVERTISER 15/01/1910/PAGE 11, 29/01/1910 PAGE 13, 5/02/1910 PAGE 5
28/02/1931 PAGE 12, 19/03/1938 PAGE 7
RAILWAY INFORMATION MR R GRIFFITHS

PHOTOGRAPH
ROTHERHAM ARCHIVES & LOCAL STUDY SERVICE
LABOUR EXCHANGE 1910 – 1920 REF 00119 PHOTOGRAPHER UNKNOWN

HOUSE OF HELP FOR GIRLS
ANNUAL REPORT 1929 ROTHERHAM ARCHIVES REF 156/T3/1
ROTHERHAM PARISH MAGAZINE 'HOMEWORDS FOR HEARTH AND HOME' 1893
KELLYS DIRECTORIES 1898 &1901

PHOTOGRAPH
ROTHERHAM ARCHIVES & LOCAL STUDY SERVICE
SMITH'S PAWN BROKERS 1903 – 1907 REF 15862 STEWART & WOLF [LMA]

Nine

The 'New' Baths

Rotherham Advertiser Artists impression of the
Opening of the New Swimming Baths 1936

THE NEW BATHS

ROTHERHAM AND MASBROUGH

PUBLIC BATHS

WESTGATE, ROTHERHAM.

Mr. **WILLIAM WRIGHT** begs to inform the Public that the above Baths, after having undergone considerable alteration and improvement, will be re-opened to the Public on the 1st day of September, 1854, at the under-mentioned reduced scale of charges, and he takes this opportunity of intimating that it is his intention to continue them as Baths if anything like a fair amount of Public support be obtained.

Prior to the day of opening the Public will be solicited to become Subscribers, and the Proprietor trusts that he shall receive such encouragement as will warrant their continuance, and that so great a Boon as Public Baths will not be lost to the neighbourhood.

Annual Subscription.	£	s	d	Single Baths.	£	s	d
One Person (three times per week) - - - -	0	15	0	Vapour - - - - -		1	0
Two of the same family, do.	1	5	0	Slipper (soap allowed) - -	0	9	
Every additional Person, (being a son or daughter) do. - - - -	0	5	0	Private, Buxton Temperature, Plunging and Douche -	0	9	
				Tepid Plunging, first class -	0	6	
Every additional inmate do. - - - - -	0	10	0	Ditto, second class - - -	0	2	
				Shower, Cold, or Tepid -	0	4	

SUBSCRIPTIONS TO BE PAID IN ADVANCE.

Subscribers will have the privilege of using any Bath in the Establishment that is disengaged.

The First Class Tepid Plunging Bath will be appropriated to the use of Ladies every day, from 9 to 12 o'clock.

Soap will be allowed in the Second Class Tepid Plunging Bath after 12 o'clock at noon, on Saturdays only.

Subscribers will be allowed two Towels to each Bath; and Non-subscribers two Towels when the charge is 6d. and upwards, but if under, only one Towel.

On a site in Westgate close to the Baths Foundry, Gummer recorded that there were 'well equipped public baths' in private ownership. It was from these that the Baths foundry derived its name.

In 1887 the Main Street Baths, or 'Old Baths' were constructed. The need for new baths became clear as the number of people using Main Street rose from 49,224 to 131,887 between 1921 and 1934. Generations of schoolchildren filed into the entrance of the old baths, rubbed the nose of the bust of Burgess, the channel swimmer and then continued through into the baths. This tradition transferred to The 'New Baths' or Sheffield Road Baths as they later became known.

1854

REF 10350

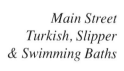

Main Street Turkish, Slipper & Swimming Baths

ROTHERHAM'S NEW SWIMMING BATH

ROTHERHAM

CORPORATION BATHS   SHEFFIELD   ROAD

SUPER SWIMMING BATH
AND DIVING POOL

SUMMER SEASON.
Swimming—
MIXED BATHING AT ALL TIMES

TIMES OF OPENING AND CLOSING:
... 7 a.m. to 10 p.m.
... 7 a.m. to 10 a.m.

CHARGES:
CHILDREN 3d. after 5 p.m. 6d.
CAFE ONLY 1d. including light Refreshment.

REFRESHMENTS CAN BE
OBTAINED AT
POPULAR PRICES
IN OUR
Modern & Well-furnished Café

Spacious CAR PARK Provided.

WINTER · SEASON
DURING THE Winter months the Bath
converted into a First Class Hall
for social functions of all descriptions. Particulars, conditions, hire charges, etc. can be obtained on
application to the Bath Superintendent

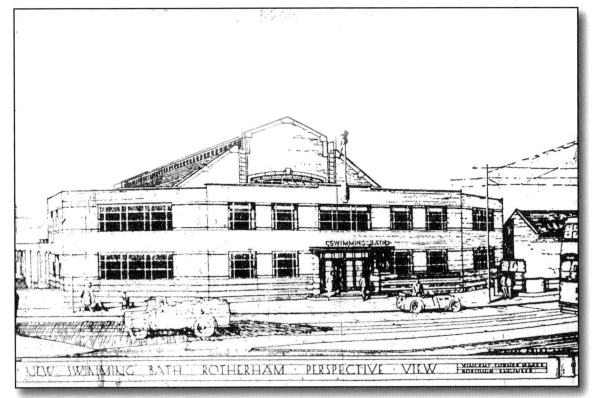

NEW SWIMMING BATH ROTHERHAM · PERSPECTIVE · VIEW

The New Baths, opened in 1936, were built at a cost of £40,835 and considered to be one of the most modern in the country. The exterior was built in red brick with a rusticated base and stone coloured terra-cotta bands.

Patrons entered the building under a canopy sited over the main entrance into an oak panelled vestibule, opening out into a cream and green tiled entrance hall.

Having obtained tickets from the oak lined pay box, patrons proceeded through into the cloakrooms. Swimmers collected a numbered rubber wristband and went to their respective changing rooms where there were 100 separately heated cubicles. Behind the dressing rooms, warm and cold showers, foot sprays and lavatories were provided.

A new feature of these baths was that no person could enter without first having passed through a footbath.

The swimming bath measured 100ft long and 40 ft wide compared with the old baths of 75ft long and 37ft wide and had a safe shallow end for non-swimmers.

Six swimming lines were marked out in the tiling on the bottom of the pool and a polo area marked out on the bath surround. Around the sides of the pool were three permanent terraces finished in terrazzo, these could be covered with canvas-covered rubber seating for spectators at galas and other functions.

The diving board at the deep end had fixed boards at four, three and one metres and two springboards at three and one metres. The main diving board could be raised to five metres for galas. The bath itself had a capacity of 24,500 cubic ft and contained 153,000 gallons of water.

The café, decorated with walnut panelled dado had windows over-looking the main street and the pool and provided seating for 80 persons at tables during the swimming season. Admittance to the café cost 4d and was offset against purchases.

In winter a portable maple floor erected on tubular steel scaffolding converted the baths hall for meetings or dances for approximately 1100 persons.

The baths continued until 2004 when they were closed down following a safety inspection. During 2005 these baths were demolished to make way for new plans for the Westgate area.

ROTHERHAM CORPORATION

BATHS ASSEMBLY HALL

SHEFFIELD ROAD ——— ROTHERHAM

Telephone 1018

THE BATHS HALL is available for Hire for DANCES, WHIST DRIVES, CONCERTS, and other Public or Private functions, etc., during the Winter months.

For Application Form and List of Charges, apply to BATHS SUPERINTENDENT, SHEFFIELD ROAD BATHS, ROTHERHAM.

Owing to heavy demand, it is essential to apply early for Bookings.

REFERENCE
ROTHERHAM ADVERTISER 25/07/1936
ILLUSTRATIONS
ROTHERHAM ADVERTISER 6/04/1935, 25/07/1936,
MAIN STREET TURKISH, SLIPPER & SWIMMING BATHS
CORONATION SOUVENIR 1937
ROTHERHAM ARCHIVES & LOCAL STUDY SERVICE
PHOTOGRAPH
PUBLIC BATHS WESTGATE 1854 REF 10350 PHOTOGRAPHER UNKNOWN

Ten

People of Westgate

REF 00151   *1903-1906*

Westgate at the junction with Main Street, looking towards All Saints Church
before the Imperial Buildings were built

John Platt II
1728-1810

John Platt the 18th century Rotherham Mason-Architect was responsible for many prestigious commissions in Rotherham and surrounding areas from 1748 until 1799.

He was born at Red House, Near Woodlaithes, Thrybergh 9th March 1728.

His father George, a Mason-Architect died in 1743 and his mother Elizabeth brought up seven children and looked after the business until John was old enough to take over.

John married Ann Fitzgerald [from Dublin] in Doncaster 1757. They had several children although none wished to follow the family tradition.

Platt was responsible for designing and building the marble staircase at Clifton House for Joshua Walker and later a marble staircase at Eastwood House. He agreed in August 1775 to build the Feoffees Charity School for the sum of £235 although the final cost was £254. The building was to be completed by Whitsuntide Sunday 1776. Other local commissions undertaken were at Wentworth Castle, Wortley Hall, Thundercliffe Grange and Ferham House.

In 1764 Platt designed and estimated for the 'Arches and Road' from Bow Bridge into the town, 'contracted and executed the same'.

Platt increased his business interests by renting quarries in Ashford. He purchased a quarter share in the Ashford Marble Works Derbyshire

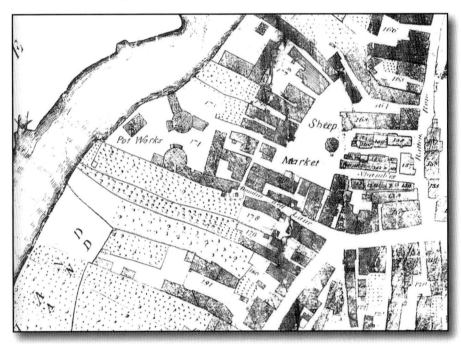

BY KIND PERMISSION OF ROTHERHAM ARCHIVES & LOCAL STUDY SERVICE

in 1765 and in later years became sole owner. During 1765 he agreed with Fenney and Wood to build a 'Pot Works' known as Rotherham Pottery on the banks of the Don. Platt entered into partnership with William Fenney but this agreement dissolved in 1766. Later that year Platt was joined by Samuel Walker Junior.

They made a Staffordshire type of white and cream-coloured earthenware and Platt travelled extensively seeking orders. In 1772 Samuel Walker Senior bought out Platt's half share in the business.

Masonry and building works remained the most important part of Platt's working life. In 1794 Platt designed and built himself a large house in Westgate with a garden 'sloping gently down to the River Don'. What remains of the house is a part of the old Co-operative Buildings, the rest was lost in the widening of Westgate and the construction of Main Street.

In 1808 Platt sold his property in Westgate. This consisted of six lots, the first of which were several tenanted dwelling houses with yard and garden.

Lot two comprised 'all that building fronting Westgate with land and ground extending to the River Don', a total of 1707sq yards in the occupation of Mr J Platt. This was sold to R Clarke for £206.

Lots three, four, and five were parcels of land called Carr Croft and lot six, one other piece of land. These were said to be also in the occupation of John Platt and adjoined the River Don.

Although Platt sold his house to R Clarke in 1808 he continued to live there until his death in December 1810. His wife Ann died August 1809 and they are interred in the family vault in Rotherham Parish Churchyard. A monument erected to their memory in All Saints Parish Church is believed to be covered by the organ in the North Transept.

A salt glazed jug inscribed John Platt 1767 was acquired by the Victoria and Albert Museum in 1970.

"The jug is beautifully painted with floral sprays in pink, green, yellow and brick red"

ROBERT SPENDLOVE

A character of the mid 1800's

The 1851 census records Spendlove aged 29 years living at 68 Westgate with his wife Mary and family. He was born in Ashlea, Derbyshire and listed as a Licensed Victualler. The son of wealthy parents, Spendlove was one of the most well known men of his day. 'He had ample funds, lived life to the full and spent money freely in entertaining such company as his buoyant spirit demanded'.

Although he was wild and reckless Spendlove never forgot he had been brought up a gentleman. He became Licensee of the Ship Hotel 1849-1852 succeeding Charles Dobb.

REF 00137 *Ship Hotel 1840*

The Ship Hotel became the centre for the wild spirits of the town and many mischievous escapades emanated from this hostelry. On one occasion Robert laid a wager for a large sum of money, that he could sit in front of the clock in the Crown bar and for one hour keep pace with the ticking of the seconds repeating the words 'here she goes, there she goes'. His wife was informed and hurried to the scene. Unable to 'move him from his purpose' she sent for a policeman and the contest was brought to an abrupt end. During the diversion Spendlove made himself scarce with the wager.

Another time he purchased a bear at York to provide fun at the Ship Hotel. Unfortunately its 'loving hugs were not appreciated by the customers and the bear had to be disposed of'.

Robert Spendlove's wife possessed good business acumen and successfully managed her husband's business interests including a butchers shop in the Shambles. Despite her watchful eye, her husband repeatedly got into trouble.

The Robinson Sisters

Two of the most well known inhabitants of Westgate in the early 1900's were Marion and Eleanor Bentley Robinson. They belonged to one of Rotherham's oldest families being the daughters of Dr [Major] E Robinson who was a third generation of medical practitioners in the town and had a surgery in Wellgate. Major Robinson was instrumental in the formation of the Rotherham Detachment 2nd V. B. York & Lancaster Regiment with Mr Arthur Hirst of The Mount and Mr George W Chambers of Clough House.

Marion and Eleanor were also the grand daughters of Robert Bentley of Bentley's Brewery. They lived at West Ville, one of three houses built alongside the Brewery, the other two being West House and Mill House.

This part of Westgate had consisted of a row of stone built and detached Villa residences and cottages and was once described as the chief residential part of Rotherham.

The Robinson sisters became known in every part of Westgate for their help and charitable giving as the area gave way to poor housing conditions and slums.

Marion supported the mission churches in Westgate and Ickles and was a devoted church worker. She was interested in the workhouse in Alma Road and a founder member of the Brabazon Society known for its work among elderly people in need. Marion was one of the founders of a club for men and boys in Westgate and over a period of twenty years conducted a bible class for the men.

Marion was Honorary Secretary of the RSPCA for forty years which she started in Rotherham with Miss B Chambers. She was also Honorary Secretary to the Missions to Seamen's Society.

Marion Bentley Robinson died in 1932 aged 76 years.

Eleanor Robinson continued working with the poor people of Westgate and the RSPCA both of which she had undertaken with her sister. By 1936 Westgate was changing, the countryside near her home was disappearing and the noise of town encroaching. Eleanor decided to leave West Ville, the family home of generations and spend her retirement in Wales, with her niece Hilda Robinson.

Members and friends gathered in Westgate Mission to pay tribute to Eleanor who was given the accolade of being the greatest church worker in Rotherham for fifty-one years. She gave loyal and faithful service to the Westgate Mission church and St Peters, Ickles. Many tributes were paid and gifts given.

In 1942 Eleanor Bentley Robinson died. She was returned to Rotherham for burial after a service in the Parish Church. Many tributes were paid to this remarkable lady.

REF 15863

Westgate
1903-1907

ROBERT MARSH 1
1824-1908

Westgate was both a residential and professional part of the town. Drakes Directory 1862 listed several Attorneys practising there. Among them were Marsh & Edwards at 8 Westgate, William Fretwell Hoyle, 20 Westgate and Thomas Vickers Favell, 30 Westgate.

Robert Marsh 1 was born in Grindleford Derbyshire and moved with his parents to live at Ickles Hall when he was five years old. The son of Robert Marsh, he was articled to William Fretwell Hoyle, became a solicitor in 1845 and eventually a partner. In 1857 he married Elizabeth [Betsy] Fernie and lived at Dalton House.

Frederick Edwards became a solicitor in 1857 and was a partner of Robert Marsh for several years.

Robert was a member of the local board of health in 1858 and became a town councillor after the incorporation of the borough in 1871.

He became an Alderman, was elected Mayor of Rotherham July 1880 following the death of the Mayor Captain Harrison and was re elected Mayor in November 1880. He served the town as Mayor, Alderman and Councillor continuously for thirty three years and was elected Feoffee in 1877 and Greave of the Common Lands of Rotherham in 1884, 1890, & 1896.

Fernie Greaves in his book 'Afterglow' described the appearance of 'Uncle Marsh' as 'short and bald with undefined wisps of white hair'. 'His eyes were small & watery, his nose, in the style of a snowman, was like a nobbly end of a carriage umbrella handle stuck into his face'. 'He was a person of the highest integrity in his professional life' and 'distinguished for kindness of disposition and geniality'.

The family tradition continued with Robert Marsh 11 1858/9-1915 who was articled to his father and became a solicitor in 1883. He partnered his father until his death and then his son Robert Preston Marsh who became a solicitor in 1913.

ARTHUR HIRST

Arthur Hirst was born near Bradford in 1821. He obtained a commission in the Army and rose to the rank of Captain. His brother-in-law Robert J Bentley persuaded him to leave the army and become manager of the brewery and estate owned by the family of Bentley's Brewery.

A house built by Robert J Bentley at the southern end of Westgate was named 'The Mount'. It was here that Arthur Hirst and his family lived from the 1850's until his death in 1900.

The census records between 1851 and 1891 reveal the extent of his household.

In 1851 there were three occupants, Arthur Hirst, his wife Margaret [who came from Dublin] and one servant.

By 1861 the household had expanded considerably.

Arthur Hirst	Head	mar	39	Maltster & Agent	Bradford
Margaret Hirst	Wife	mar	31		Dublin
Arthur E Hirst	Son		9	Scholar	Rotherham
Alice Hirst	Dau		8	Scholar	Rotherham
Walter Hirst	Son		7	Scholar	Rotherham
Gertrude E Hirst	Dau		6	Scholar	Rotherham
Alfred LP Hirst	Son		4	Scholar	Rotherham
Margaret Hirst	Dau		8mths		Rotherham
Joseph Hirst	Bro	mar	35	Brewer	Bradford
Ann Brown	Serv	unmar	27	Cook	Rotherham
Martha Nicholson	Serv	unmar	23	Housemaid	Birmingham
Mary Johnson	Serv	unmar	20	Nurse	Loughborough

In 1871 the household expanded even more to fourteen. Some children disappeared and were replaced by four new additions. The staff changed and had a different Cook, two housemaids and a Laundress. Also visiting was Marie JE Fauve aged 22 an Artiste from France.

Ten years later in 1881 more children left home and the household contracted to nine. They employed one housemaid, Cook and Laundress.

Household members contracted again to seven on the 1891 census and domestic help was reduced to a cook/domestic and housemaid.

Arthur Hirst died in January 1900 aged 78 years and is buried in Moorgate Cemetery. Their records show him as 'Gentleman'.

The home of the Hirst family for nearly fifty years 'The Mount' continued to be remembered.

In 1921/2 Bentley's Brewery attempted unsuccessfully to sell the house to the Guardians of the Poor. By the 1930's the house appeared to be in multiple occupancy and became a lodging house in 1935.

Inspection of the premises in 1937 showed 1 family and 13 male lodgers.
The property was again inspected in January 1938 and living there were a family paying 11/- per week and 15 male lodgers each paying 7/- weekly including Sunday dinner and laundry. 'The premises were well furnished and bedding clean'.

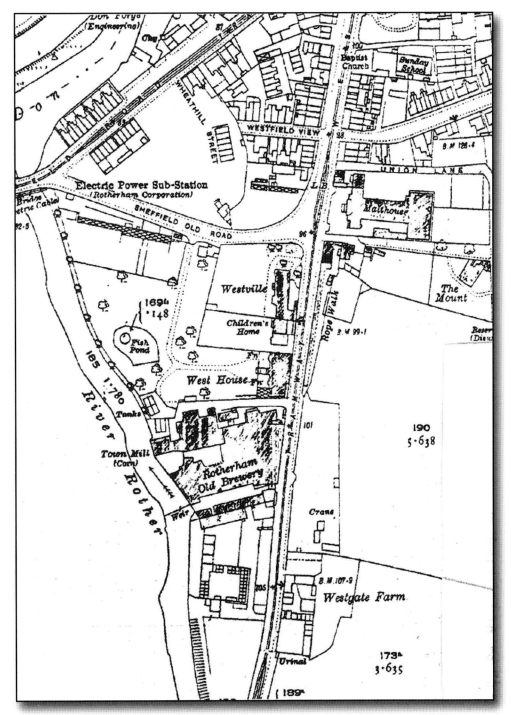

In 1937 The Public Assistance Committee considered acquiring the land and premises for a recreation ground for the residents of the Alma Road Institution. They purchased both for approx £1000. The house, which consisted of 16 rooms, an attic and three cellars was demolished in 1939.

The name of the house was destined to continue when in 1943 authorities were looking for a new name for the 'Alma Road Institution'. This became 'The Mount' and continued as part of Moorgate Hospital until closure and eventual demolition when the name disappeared again.

JOHN SIMPSON

'Rotherham Character'

known as Johnny Simpson and Tinny Simpson

John Simpson grew up in a family consisting of seven boys and two girls. His father died at the age of 52 years and as his brothers and sisters left home John decided to stay and look after his mother. Isabella. He remained a bachelor for the rest of his life.

John and his mother ran a lodging house in Westgate and men in need never went without a nights lodging or a good meal. He proved a good friend to victims of the depression in the early 1930's when 'every copper counted' and enabled supplies of food and tea to be available in small quantities for only a few pence.

His mother was a devout Christian who earned the respect of townsfolk for her kindness to the poor. After her death John erected a shrine as a memorial to her. The continental shrine was built against the gable of the lodging house with a light shining down into the yard after nightfall.

John started up in business as an Antique dealer and his shop fronted the Lodging house. He had articles of every description, china, pewter ware, crystal chandeliers, curios, brass and copper warmers. Many weird and wonderful things found its way into the shop.

In his backyard were to be found other articles of antique value surrounded by mirrors, marble busts, ornaments and flowerpots. In addition to these, marble statues were let into the wall overlooking a yard full of livestock, geese, chickens, dogs and at one time as many as 100 fantail pigeons.

John Simpson was devoted to his mother and continued the lodging house as a living memorial to her. He was a reserved man who preferred his own company other than that of his dogs and lodging house friends. He smoked and drank little. His business was very important to him and gave him much pleasure. He was known as a generous man and gave away many of the oddly assorted curios and antiques he acquired.

He died in 1953 and was buried in Moorgate cemetery following a service by Bishop Gerard.

OLD ANTIQUE SHOPPE will buy your old BRASS and COPPER WARE, ANTIQUE FURNITURE ONLY. POT FIGURES, VASES, LUSTRES. Good Prices Paid. Call, send p.c. or phone Rotherham 2523. SIMPSON'S, 44, WESTGATE, ROTHERHAM. Est. 1882. e5849

The Oddfellows

In June 1898 the opening of the Oddfellows Hall was quite an occasion. The celebrations were held over two days, the first on Sunday afternoon when a procession headed by Whiston Brass Band and musicians from Greasbro' paraded to the Parish Church for a service.

The following day the formal ceremony of the opening of the Hall was performed by the Grand Master of the Order, Thomas Edmondson and supported by the Mayor and other dignitaries.

For twenty-five years the members of the Independent Order of Oddfellows [Manchester Unity] Friendly Society had been looking for premises for their business and social activities but it was not until 1898 that this could be put into effect. A few months earlier the old County Court offices in Westgate were offered for sale.

RFHS COLIN LEONARD 1965

The Oddfellows purchased the offices and six dilapidated cottages including an area of garden at the back of the premises at an auction sale for £1410.

Considerable alterations were made to the building to provide a suite of rooms and the erection of eight cottages including a caretaker's residence.

The ground floor of the building consisted of four shops which were rented out. The upper storey had a concert hall capable of seating 300 people, two large lodge rooms, billiard, games, smoke and reading rooms at a total cost of £4557.

The Rotherham Annual 1903 described it as 'A fine building of great importance to friendly societies with ample accommodation provided at a reasonable charge for Lodge or General meetings of Friendly Societies'.

Westgate ladies outside The Wellington Inn Circa 1910

From left to right: Mrs Emily Florence Smith furniture broker of 50 Westgate, Mrs Mills and baby, Mrs Curtis from the lodging house at 44 Westgate, Mrs Nancy Walker nee Round in her early 20's. Mrs Mills the landlady standing at the back.

Phomena, Annie, Harry, Hannah, Emily Sarah, Ethel & Elsie
Family members who loved to dress up, perform and hold concerts on a stage behind the lodging house at 6 Sheffield Road,

Circa 1910

Sitting in the 'pram of the day' is Muriel Edwards outside her home at 33 Coke Lane, Westgate

REFERENCE
FRONTISPIECE PHOTOGRAPH
ROTHERHAM ARCHIVES & LOCAL STUDY SERVICE
WESTGATE JUNCTION/MAIN STREET REF 00151 1903-1906
PHOTOGRAPHER UNKNOWN

JOHN PLATT
ROTHERHAM ARCHIVES & LOCAL STUDY SERVICE
JOHN PLATT LETTERS AND JOURNAL REF 101/F

POTTS JD PLATT OF ROTHERHAM 1959
LAWRENCE HEATHER YORKSHIRE POTS AND POTTERIES 1974
ELLIOTT BRIAN ARCHITECTS OF NO SLENDER MERIT: PLATT
OF ROTHERHAM 1700-1810 CHAPTER 7 ASPECTS OF
ROTHERHAM 3 1998

ROBERT SPENDLOVE
GUMMER G REMINISCENCES OF ROTHERHAM 1927
1851 CENSUS RECORDS [ROTHERHAM ARCHIVES & LOCAL
STUDY SERVICE]

THE ROBINSON SISTERS
ROTHERHAM ADVERTISER 6/12/1932,
21/4/1945,8/2/1936,16/5/1936,18/4/1942.

ARTHUR HIRST
ROTHERHAM ARCHIVES & LOCAL STUDY SERVICE
CENSUS RECORDS 1851-1891
IVANHOE REVIEW SPRING 1993 F CROWDER
WESTGATE CLEARANCE FILES 1937/8

ROBERT MARSH
J.H. COCKBURN ROTHERHAM LAWYERS DURING 350 YEARS
1932
ROTHERHAM ADVERTISER 17/07/1880, 13/11/1880, 9/05/1908.
FERNIE GREAVES BOOK 'AFTERGLOW' 1966 PT/ PAGE 31/32
Reproduced by kind permission of Mrs EA Holmes

JOHN SIMPSON
ROTHERHAM ADVERTISER 10/10/1953, 17/10/1953

THE ODDFELLOWES
ROTHERHAM ADVERTISER 25/06/1898 page 3
ROTHERHAM ANNUAL 1903

PHOTOGRAPHS
SALT GLAZED JUG 1767 JOHN PLATT

ROTHERHAM ARCHIVES & LOCAL STUDY SERVICE
PHOTOGRAPH SHIP HOTEL 1840 REF 00137
PHOTOGRAPHER UNKNOWN
PHOTOGRAPH WESTGATE 1903-1907
PHOTOGRAPHER G W KNAPTON REF 15863 LMA
MAP ROTHERHAM POTTERY [POT WORKS]
MAP 'THE MOUNT'

ROBERT MARSH REMINISCENCES OF ROTHERHAM GUMMER
G 1927
PART PHOTOGRAPH - PHOTOGRAPHER UNKNOWN

RFHS
THE ODDFELLOWS HALL 1965 PHOTOGRAPHER COLIN
LEONARD

WESTGATE 1910. OUTSIDE THE WELLINGTON INN
Reproduced by kind permission of Mr Roy Creamer

33 COKE LANE & 6 SHEFFIED ROAD
Reproduced by kind permission of Nancy Edwards

ADVERTISEMENT
OLD ANTIQUE SHOPPE SIMPSON'S ROTHERHAM ADVERTISER
25/04/1953 PGE 2

Eleven

Westgate Snippets

Extracts of Westgate from:

Reminiscences of G.Gummer

'Ye Olde Rotherham Town'

by William Oakley

&

Articles from

The Rotherham Advertiser

Extracts of Westgate from

'Reminiscences of Rotherham' by G Gummer

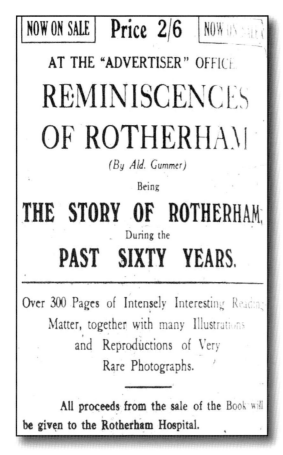

NOW ON SALE Price **2/6** NOW ON SALE

AT THE "ADVERTISER" OFFICE

REMINISCENCES
OF ROTHERHAM
(By Ald. Gummer)

Being

THE STORY OF ROTHERHAM,

During the

PAST SIXTY YEARS.

Over 300 Pages of Intensely Interesting Reading Matter, together with many Illustrations and Reproductions of Very Rare Photographs.

All proceeds from the sale of the Book will be given to the Rotherham Hospital.

Gummer described an idyllic picture difficult to comprehend today.

Westgate was known as a good residential district. 'Many of the houses on the western side of the 'gate' had gardens extending to the river. The banks were green and hawthorn trees in spring were covered with fragrant blossom, providing shade and shelter on the hottest day'.

In summertime George Thompson of Water Lane, Westgate hired out pleasure boats and rowing was enjoyed for several miles up river. Bathing took place in the clear waters of the River Rother and Bromley Sands near Bow Bridge was a popular area for the youngsters of Westgate.

Gummer recalled the time when the life of Edward Prince of Wales was in imminent danger and bulletins were posted in many public places. Locally they were exhibited in the windows of the Old Post Office Westgate. This site later became the Co-operative Stores.

Rotherham Race Meetings

Mr G A Wilson and associates were responsible for the inauguration of Hunt Races in 1889. On race days the thoroughfare from Westgate station to the course at Broom were crowded with pleasure seekers.

Mrs Mather

Adjoining the Three Cranes in High Street, Mrs Mather was in business as a Hatter. She was known as a 'precise, prim, old lady' whose daughter married a Mr Bingham, provision merchant of Westgate. The wedding was remembered because the churchyard was decorated with 'red druggetting'.

In another shop adjacent to The Three Cranes, High Street, the Brettell brothers Francis and Morris, sons of the Minister of The Old Chapel, Downs Row had a Stationary Business. They were responsible for editing one of the first Pitman Shorthand manuals and wrote letters and valentines for their customers.

In contrast;

Tosh Rylands was known as the 'Terror of the town'. He was a 'tall, lanky, bony and boisterous man' who lived in Westgate.

Tosh was often to be found in 'quarrelsome mood' due to drink and the police would not approach him single-handed.

On the several occasions he was taken into custody it required six policemen to restrain him. After forcing him into a cab he was known to kick the sides of the vehicle out!

REFERENCE

'DRUGGET'

COARSE WOOLLEN MATERIAL USED FOR FLOOR OR TABLE COVERING. AN OVERCARPET

Westgate Snippets from his journal
'Ye Olde Rotherham Town' by William Oakley

Wlliam Oakley recorded jottings of everyday life and gave an insight into life at that time. The extracts relating to Westgate are not in chronological order but are shown as they appear in his book.

1880

Richard Hague kept the Little Swann 1865-1868 and was the last landlord. The Little Swann was changed into a lodging house and furniture shop. When Hague left Westgate he went to live at College Lane where he kept a lodging house. He weighed 20 stone and it took twelve men to lift him when he died. The Little Swann was demolished.

1830

The family of Bentley was very large and lived at West End. At one time there was a cannon fired at 10pm each night at Bentley's Brewery.

1872

James Hattersley, Rope Maker, lived and died in Westgate

1874

John Hanby, Grocer and Provisions Dealer. He had two wives and his shop was in Westgate.

1872

Richard Lomas, Grocer & Provisions Dealer lived in Westgate and was very good to the poor.

1850

Favell of Oil Mill Fold—Nailmaker

1860

Henry Taylor was schoolmaster of the Hollis School for many years. He was small in stature, a violinist and died a 'good old age' in Copeland Place.

1865

John Evans had a Hairdressers shop in Westgate

1869

James Hodgeson—A Miller who lived at the Mill House, Westgate.

1870

George Appleyard— Miller at Canklow House. 'The Mill was taken down'.

1868

William A Bingham — A Grocery & Provisions Dealer at the bottom of Westgate

1880

Harris Iron Foundry in Westgate

1841

'Ye Old Town Nailmakers'

William Favell   Westgate

John Gordon   ,,

Joseph Wilkinson   ,,

Dickinson   ,,

James & John Woodhead – Starch & Gum Maker Westgate

1790

The Travellers Inn Westgate closed 1910 and the last landlord was named King.

1880

Joseph Hutton was landlord of the Little Swan 1861-1864. He died aged 65 years. The last landlord was Richard Hague 1865-1868.

1860

John Booth — Curriers and Leather Dressers in College Street and lived in Westgate

1873

Charles Yates — Grocers and Dealers Westgate- Next to The Old Post Office. Now demolished.

1882

Thomas Steer — Fish Dealer Westgate

1879

Henry Steer — Coal Dealer Westgate

1878

Thompson — Milk Dealer Westgate Green

1868

Howson — Milk Dealer Westgate

1869

Astbury – Salt Dealer at the back of the Dusty Miller who went round with a horse and cart for several years and lived in Westgate.

Benjamin Parker of Man Place Westgate was a Miller who had six sons and three daughters

1869

William Nicholson – Plumber & Glazier who worked for Bentley's Brewery for many years and died 'a good old age'. He had five sons, two daughters and lived in Alma Road. He died in 1920 aged 85 years.

1841

George Brookes — Carrier, supplied Poultry, Butter, Eggs Fruit and Potatoes from Lincolnshire Market. His shop was in Westgate where Oxley & Coward was later situated.

The Old Cutlers Arms in Westgate dated back to 1700 and was demolished for a new one to be built in its place.

1860

Thomas Linton lived in Westgate and both he and his wife were Nailmakers. They had a large family.

A family by the name of Shaw lived by Coke Lane and sold old furniture.

1870

John Goodlad – 'A little old man' who lived in Water Lane and was a timekeeper and warehouseman at the Stove Grate Works.

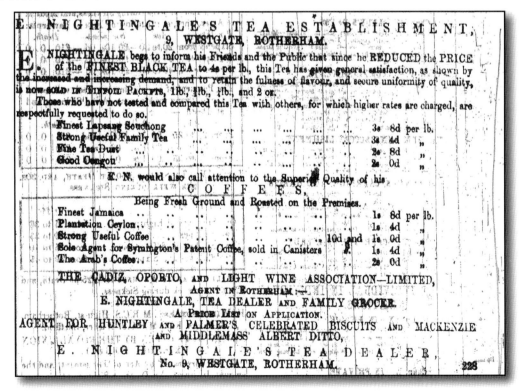

William Oakley remarked in his journal that Edward Nightingale was a very old name in Rotherham and he was a Grocer & Provisions Dealer who had a Candle Works in Main Street and a house and shop in Westgate.

An article in the Rotherham Advertiser 1950 'Reminiscences of an earlier time' gave an insight into inhabitants of Westgate in the mid 19th century.

'Westgate, not to the west by compass point, but to the West End—The residential and professional end of the old town'.

In 1833 Westgate had Attorneys, an Auctioneer, the Sheriffs Officer and two Veterinary Surgeons living there.

By 1861 there was a private teaching academy situated at 81 Westgate, the Hollis charity school in Oil Mill Fold and an eating and coffee house at 40 Westgate. Robert John Bentley 'Maltster and Brewer of ale and porter' resided with his family adjacent to Bentley's Brewery.

The town's population was 8389 and there were eight 'gentlemen' recorded. This title had nothing to do with manners or morals, but indicated that they were under no obligation to work for a living. Two of these gentlemen resided in Westgate, Edward Pagdin at 43 Westgate and Edward Robinson, Surgeon who practiced from West Ville.

B. C. WILLIAMS,

No. 37, Westgate, Rotherham,

BEGS TO INFORM THE PUBLIC THAT THE ABOVE PREMISES

ARE NOW OPEN

FOR THE

MEDICO-BOTANIC PRACTICE,

Which is now gaining the attention and support of thousands. As an art it is honest and straightforward in its administration, safe in its effects, and radical in the cure. Passing by the poisonous, and therefore dangerous properties of the mineral agents, he has a herb, which, after dislodging the enemy, leaves no residue that shall afflict the patient or fill the pockets of a monoplising faculty. Common sense would argue that the field or meadow from which we reap our every-day food, and so wisely adapted for the sustenance of life, is the place alone from which we may seek restoratives for the weak, or medicine for the disease.
12

In 1862 Benjamin C. Williams lived at 37 Westgate and practised as a medico- botanic practitioner During 1871 there were two accountants, three architects and surveyors, five attorneys, nine Fire and Life assurance officers, brick and tile manufacturers, coach builder, dentist, wheelwright and surgeon. Despite the number of small workshops, Westgate was essentially a residential and professional west end.

The following advertisement appeared in the Rotherham and Masbrough Advertiser on 28th March 1868 and is reproduced to give an insight into the household effects of the day.

SALE BY MR WADDY

NO 44 WESTGATE ROTHERHAM

VALUABLE HOUSEHOLD FURNITURE AND EFFECTS

Mr Waddy is honoured with instructions from the executors of the late Mrs Wigfield to Sell by Auction on Thursday 2nd April 1868 as above, the whole of the very well made DINING, DRAWING, and BEDROOM FURNITURE, VESTIBULE, KITCHEN and other requisites.

In the Dining and Drawing rooms are excellent Mahogany Telescope Dining Table with two leaves, Mahogany Loo Table with bold pillar and claw, Mahogany Chiffonier, single and arm Mahogany chairs in hair, Mahogany Lounge Chairs in hair, Walnut Pianoforte 6 ½ Octaves, by Clarke and Boothby, London. Chimney Glass in gilt frame, plate 46"by 40", Brussells Scotch and other Carpets, Hearth Rugs, Mahogany Pole Fire Screen, Bronze Fenders with polished Mountings, Ashes Pans with loose Polished Bars, Polished Steel Fire Irons with Bronzed Mountings, neat Three light Gaselier, Mahogany Butler's Tray and Stand etc, etc.

The Bedroom appointments, Half Tester Mahogany Bedsteads with massive footboards, Cornices, Rods and Rings, clad with Moreen and Union Damask

44 Westgate appears on the far right of the picture

hangings, Camp and other Bedsteads upholstered with Union, Damask and other hangings, Hair Mattresses, Feather Beds, Bolsters and Pillows, Painted Wardrobe and Drawers, Mahogany Chest of Drawers, Mahogany Dressing Tables, large Mahogany Dressing Glass, Mahogany Bedsteps and night commode, Painted Dressing Chest with Cupboards and Drawers, Painted Wash and Dressing Tables, Mahogany Bed Ottomans, Napkin Rails Toilet Services, Cain and Rush seated Chairs, Fenders and Fire Irons, Window Cornices and Poles with Drapery, Venetian and Gauze Blinds , Easy Chair, Birch stand, Time Piece etc.

The Vestibule, Kitchen and other requisites, Mahogany and Oak Hat and Umbrella Stands, Dresser, Round and Square Tables, Chairs, Block Tin Dish Covers, Copper, Brass and Iron Pans, Dinner and Tea Services, Marble Pastry slab, Cut Glass, a large assortment of Earthenware and general assemblage of Culinary and other utensils, also Capital Invalid's Bath Chair in good condition, upholstered in Green American cloth, with loose Apron and Cushions.

On View on Wednesday April 1st, from Ten to four, and on the Morning of the Sale

Sale at Half- past Ten o'clock precisely

In 1927 an assistant working in Mr Bewley's Newsagents shop at 31Westgate had a narrow escape as:

'LORRY GOES SHOPPING'

'Danger of Collapse after Building Framework Weakens'.

Ref 17901 EL SCRIVENS 172/104

Thick planks of wood were introduced to prevent the collapse of Mr Bewley's Newsagent's shop in Westgate after a five-ton motor lorry ran into it.

The lorry owned by E. Matthewman, haulage contractor of Balby, Doncaster and driven by Thomas Hattersley of Doncaster had been left outside a nearby public house. The driver of a tram noticed that the lorry was fouling the lines and called out for it to be moved. The lorry driver's labourer, William Bradley aged 19 of Low Road Balby, Doncaster who was seated in the vehicle started the engine and drove the lorry forward. It ran straight on and crashed into the side window of Mr Bewley's shop.

Miss Nellie Walker who was standing in the doorway dressing the window had a narrow escape from serious injury. The vehicle missed her by less than three feet.

The collision had shaken the framework of that side of the building, and it was feared it would collapse, bringing down the brickwork and masonry of the upper storey. This was avoided when wooden beams were introduced as a temporary measure to prop up the structure once the lorry hade been dragged out with chains.

The brickwork under the window had been weakened and was entirely rebuilt.

DURING 1929 RESIDENTS WERE ALARMED BY THE STRANGE APPEARANCE OF 'GHOSTS' IN WESTGATE.

Crowds of excited people gathered because of the supposed appearance of a 'ghost or ghosts' in one of the courts near the junction of Westgate and Sheffield Road. Some of the residents of the neighbourhood were concerned 'more by what they were expecting to see, than what they had seen'.

Occupiers of one of the courts spoke of uncanny experiences. One person talked about 'an apparition in white of what appeared to be an old man, who beckoned to her', while another described an 'eerie thing draped in white which fluttered across the river Don'.

Another person ridiculed the whole event and laughingly recalled a similar ghost scare of thirty years earlier.

The "ghost's" first appearance – 'the fluttering one, that is' had been seen the previous week.

'Several people were looking over the yard wall watching the firework display on Millmoor football ground," said a resident of one of the courts, when 'the thing seemed to come out of a hole near the river and had neither head nor legs. It was just a body with wings, and seemed to fly. It dodged about on waste ground for some time, and then disappeared through the big doors of an old building'.

A probable explanation of the visitation was the story that a swan had been seen in the vicinity.

Burrells Row was the scene of two incidents, the first occurred in 1896:

'THE SENSATIONAL DROWNING CASE
OF WILLIAM DRINKALL'

William Drinkall aged 17 years lost his life whilst rescuing the six year old child of a neighbour. Drinkall worked at Thomas Charles, Coach Builder, Sheffield Road and lived in Burrells Row Westgate. Father, John Drinkall identified his son at an inquest held at The Cutlers Arms Westgate.

Mr John Mason who lived at 20 Burrells Row gave evidence at the inquest stating that he heard 'an alarm' and ran to the River Don which flowed past the bottom of the Row. There he saw William Drinkall and the child struggling in the water. The child was rescued but Mason was unable to save Drinkall who could not swim. Efforts were made to revive Drinkall without success and a verdict of accidental death was recorded. Concern was raised over the poor safety measures in place by the river.

Henry Blanchard of The White Hart Hotel thought that had William Drinkall lived he would probably have been awarded the Royal Humane Society's Medal and a fund was started to erect a memorial over his grave.

Drinkall who was a member of the select class at Talbot Lane Sunday School was interred in Moorgate Cemetery in the presence of 1000 people.

The following week the mother of the child wrote to the Advertiser stating that too much credit had been given to Mr Mason and the saving of the child's life was due to William Drinkall.

The second incident happened some years later in 1913 and received the following headlines:

HOUSE FALLS INTO RIVER
SUDDEN COLLAPSE IN WESTGATE

One Sunday evening in May 1913 a house in Burrell's Row Westgate collapsed and the gable end fell into the River Don. The house, at the end of Burrell's Row, was fortunately empty being one of several closed under a Council order. The adjacent properties were inhabited and worried residents decided to leave their homes for the night in case their premises were affected by the collapse. A peculiar noise was heard from the house followed by several tons of brick and debris and a portion of the boundary wall [erected along the riverbank a few years earlier] falling into the river.

Many cracks were visible in the brickwork of the part of the house left standing and a huge crack appeared across the roadway, showing that the foundations had given way. This was thought to be due to recent heavy rain.

The collapse attracted a large crowd and police had difficulty in keeping people at a safe distance. A second fall appeared imminent and the premises were guarded until the structure could be wholly demolished. Fortunately no one was injured.

REFERENCE

FRONTISPIECE PHOTOGRAPH
PAUL FOX COLLECTION
E L SCRIVENS REF 172/102

GUMMER G REMINISCENCES OF ROTHERHAM 1927
OAKLEY WILLIAM   YE OLDE ROTHERHAM TOWN 1915
REMINISCENCES AN EARLIER TIME ROTHERHAM ADVERTISER 11/03/1950
ROTHERHAM & MASBROUGH ADVERTISER 28/03/1868
ROTHERHAM ADVERTISER 4/07/1896, 17/05/1913, 11/06/1927,/27/04/1929

ROTHEHAM FAMILY HISTORY SOCIETY
44 WESTGATE [PT] PHOTOGRAPHER COLIN LEONARD

ROTHERHAM ARCHIVES & LOCAL STUDY SERVICE
BEWLEYS SHOP E L SCRIVENS 172/104 REF 17901
BROMLEY SANDS POSTCARD LOANED BY DAVID & JOHN CLENNELL

ADVERTISEMENTS
ROTHERHAM ADVERTISER
REMINISCENCES 11/06/1927
E NIGHTINGALE 18/03/1865

DRAKES DIRECTORY 1862
MEDICO BOTANIC

Thomas Allport 1850

View of Rotherham taken from Bromley Sands

Gummer described Bromley Sands, near Bow Bridge
"as a popular area for the youngsters of Westgate"

Twelve

Westgate Revival 1950

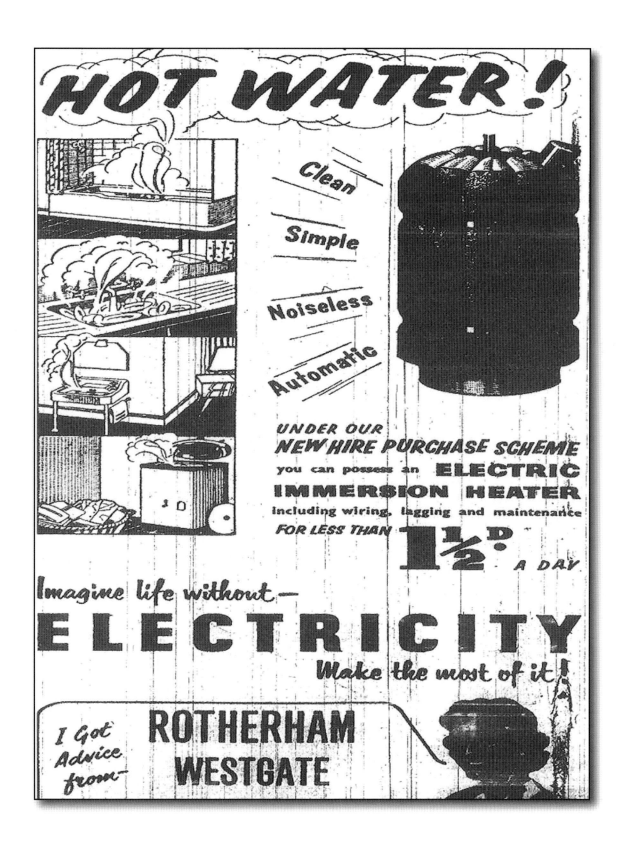

The Rotherham Advertiser reported on a Westgate Revival stating that 'Modern Westgate at that time retained little of its ancient character and its development was shown in the advertisements of the day'.

In 1896 the premises of the Co-operative Society were occupied by five private traders and two solicitors.

On the western side of the gate, the newsagents business of A Bewley and Co, was established.

Mr Bewley recorded seventy-four years service and he continued to retain an active interest in the business.

J Clayton and Sons, the Motor House, was established in Westgate in 1921, having acquired the site previously occupied by a retail shop and a lodging house. They were known in the trade as the 100 per cent Austin Dealers and carried an extensive stock of spares.

On the eastern side;

The Ship Inn had been replaced by R J Stokes and Co, whose products were in great demand.

The Electricity Board showrooms were staffed by 'local salesmen ready to advise on all matters electrical'.

Smith Bros Ltd Wholesale Electrical business was managed by R.M. Nicholson and M.A. Wilson.

A Denham and Son had a long family connection in the pottery, glass and china business. Mr Denham was the grandson of the principal of Hawley Brothers who in 1896 were noted as 'manufacturers of plain and ornamental earthenware' at the old Northfield pottery.

The Halifax building provided 'additional dignity' to the architecture of new Westgate.

The Society's 'services to the thrifty prospective house purchasers were highly appreciated'.

Handley's, Westgate served the small shopkeeper in town and district for more than forty years; their fishing tackle department stocked everything required by the complete angler, and their annual match provided the highlight of the fishing season.

Over a number of years Dean and Dawson had provided a valued service of information regarding travel facilities by road, rail, sea, and air, and their conducted tours became increasingly popular.

A Broomhead supplied boots and clogs for seventeen years to workers in the heavy industries and his safety boots were known to give excellent foot protection.

J France Ltd, established in Millgate more than 50 years ago transferred to larger premises in Oil Mill Fold, Westgate, and their products were distributed widely in South Yorkshire.

C Riley provided Rotherham with an efficient and reliable motor-coach service for many years. Sportsmen and workers appreciated the value of the travel facilities available all year round

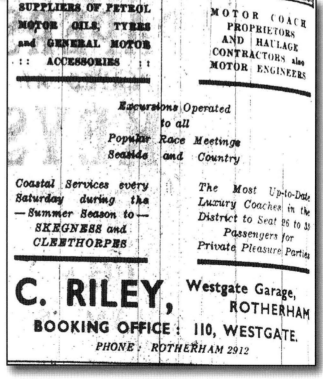

'Chas Miles for Carpets' denoted a specialist of long experience. Although carpets were in short supply, a comprehensive range of all kinds of floor coverings was always in stock.

The carpet-making department provided a much appreciated and economical service.

Well known funeral directors Messrs Parkinson & Sons was founded in the 1870's by Mr Edward Parkinson at premises in Oil Mill Fold. He is listed in Kelly's Directory 1901 as a joiner and undertaker at 10 Leopard Terrace and his home at 44 Westgate. Edward moved to 50 Westgate in 1906 and his son Joseph moved back into Oil Mill Fold in 1935. Grandson of Edward, John Lawrence joined the family business after leaving school and worked there until his death in 1971.

Other shops in business in the 1950's were John Stacey, Barber, at 36 Westgate and The Reliable Leather Stores at 40 Westgate who sold clogs for men working in the steel industry. Pieces of leather cut to size for repair work and segs and tacks [measured with a scoop into small white triangular paper bags] were also available for purchase, the business run by the Edwards family.

Westgate's Modern Food Factory

OUR MODERN HYGIENIC BAKERY—Built to meet the increased demands for our HIGH QUALITY PRODUCTS

PORK PIES, MEAT PIES, SAUSAGES and ROLLS. POTTED MEATS (in dainty cartons) PRESSED BEEF and PORK and DELICIOUS BACON FOR OUR REGISTERED CUSTOMERS.

A. E. Cooper, Ltd. THE PORK BUTCHERS 92, WESTGATE, R'HAM

REF 12862

One of the most well known businesses in Westgate was A.E. Cooper, Pork Butcher. People came from far and wide to buy their pork pies. Cooper's also had a pork manufacturing business in premises at the rear of the shop.

They supplied pork pies, sausages, stuffing and black pudding to shops in Rotherham. At Christmas time customers would be seen queuing out on the pavement to buy their pork pies.

Mr A Cooper started the family tradition in 1913 and was still serving customers until his death in 1969. His son John began working for his father as a barrow boy in 1928 and retired in 1986 after working at the Westgate shop since his youth. The business, continued by his son David was finally sold to a joint concern Wildmead Ltd.

REFERENCE

WESTGATE REVIVAL 1950- ROTHERHAM ADVERTISER 11/03/1950

HANDLEY'S ROTHERHAM ADVERTISER 25/04/1953

PARKINSON FUNERAL DIRECTORS, ROTHERHAM ADVERTISER 18/04/1953, 25/04/1953, 15/09/1962, 7/08/1971, 27/05/1994,

KELLY'S DIRECTORY 1901,1935,

AE COOPER-ROTHERHAM ADVERTISER 1/02/1969, 31/10/1986

ADVERTISEMENTS

ROTHERHAM ARCHIVES & LOCAL STUDY SERVICE

ROTHERHAM ADVERTISER 11/03/1950

ELECTRICITY

ROTHERHAM CO-OPERATIVE SOCIETY LTD

A BEWLEY & CO

J CLAYTON & SONS

R J STOKES

HALIFAX BUILDING SOCIETY

H. HANDLEY & SON LTD

DEAN & DAWSON

A.BROOMHEAD

JOSEPH FRANCE LTD

C. RILEY

CHAS J MILES

J PARKINSON

A E COOPER LTD REF 12862 PHOTOGRAPHER ROTHERHAM ADVERTISER

I hope you have enjoyed this
journey back in time.
Westgate now awaits the
next chapter in its history.

Acknowledgements

Metropolitan Borough Council of Rotherham Archives & Local Study Service, Central Library.

Sarah Wickham & Staff for their kind permission to use Archive material and their patience and help throughout this project.

Mr Doug Melloy Editor Rotherham Advertiser, Rotherham Family History Society,

Paul Fox, CC Hall, Jim Clarke, Jack Parnham, Ron Bye, The Minster Church, The Baptist Church, Rev Sean Adair, Methodist Circuit, Hollis Trustees, Paul Satterthwaite, Mrs EA Holmes, S L Smith, W Ryan, H Turner, R Griffiths, W Mapplebeck, Hickmotts Solicitors, M Kennedy, John Jackson.

Bibliography

Drakes Directory of Rotherham 1862

Guest John Historic Notices of Rotherham 1879

Blazeby WM Rev Rotherham Old Meeting House & its Ministers 1906

Oakley William Ye Olde Rotherham Town 1915

Cater PM So Great a Cloud of Witnesses 1983

Gummer G Reminiscences Of Rotherham 1927

Morley C The Stove Grate, Range, & Decorative Cast Industry of Rotherham Chapter 11 Aspects of Rotherham 3 1998

Hall CC Rotherham & District Transport Vol 1 1996

Smith Howard A History of Roads & Transport 1992

Lumb Geoff The Heyday of the Bus 1996

Hill Norman Postal History of Rotherham 1960

The Feoffees of the Common Lands [Booklet]

Satterthwaite Paul Rotherham Town Public Houses 1820-1990 1991

Munford Tony From Slums to Council Houses; The Rotherham Experience Chapter 15 Aspects of Rotherham 1995

Platt John Letters & Journal ref 101/F Rotherham Archives & Local Study Service

Potts JD Platt of Rotherham, Mason Architect 1700-1810 1959

Lawrence Heather Yorkshire Pot & Potteries 1974

Elliott Brian Architects of No Slender Merit: Platt of Rotherham 1700-1810 Chapter 7 Aspects of Rotherham 3 1998

Cockburn JH Rotherham Lawyers during 350 Years 1932

Greaves Fernie 'Afterglow' 1966

Illustrations Acknowledgement

Every effort has been made to contact or trace copyright holders. The Publishers will be glad to make good any errors or omissions brought to our attention in future editions. We are grateful to the following for permission to reproduce illustrative material:

Rotherham Archives & Local Study Service, Rotherham Advertiser, Rotherham Family History Society, Paul Fox, SL Smith, W Ryan, H Turner, Jim Clarke, Roy Creamer, CC Hall, Nancy Edwards,

Photographs

Rotherham Archives & Local Study Service from their collection:

Mainly unknown photographers with the exception of

Henry Tomlinson ref 01596 Crosby, J Leadbeater, James Smiths Pawnbrokers ref 15862 Stewart & Wolf

Westgate Baptist Chapel PH Slater Hillsborough ref unknown

Bewley's Shop ref 17901 EL Scrivens 107/104

View of Rotherham from Bromley Sands by Thomas Allport 1850 postcard loaned by David & John Clennell.

David Kenyon - The Piano Centre

Westgate Baptist Chapel Frontispiece

Rotherham Family History Society [RFHS]

& Collection of Colin Leonard

Paul Fox from his Transport collection

Westgate EL Scrivens ref 107/102

W Ryan   HET 513 & H Turner HET 512/HET514

S L Smith Single Ended Tram

John Platt 1767 Jug, Victoria & Albert Museum

Westgate Ladies Wellington Inn 1910 Roy Creamer

33 Coke Lane/6 Sheffield Road 1910 Nancy Edwards

Maps

Rotherham Archives & Local Study Service

Rotherham Regional Planning Scheme 1925 WR Davidge

Pot Works Rotherham Pottery

Westgate/Canklow Road

VIEW OF ROTHERHAM, YORKSHIRE.

Thomas Allport 1850